The Car-Keeper's Guide

The Car-Keeper's Guide

James Joseph

Contemporary Books, Inc.
Chicago

Library of Congress Cataloging in Publication Data

Joseph, James.
   The car-keeper's guide.

   Includes index.
   1. Automobiles—Maintenance and repair.   I. Title.
TL152.J67   629.28'722   81-69602
ISBN 0-8092-5855-2   AACR2

All illustrations, unless otherwise indicated, are courtesy of James Joseph.

Published by Contemporary Books, Inc.
180 North Michigan Avenue, Chicago, Illinois 60601
Manufactured in the United States of America
Library of Congress Catalog Card Number: 81-69602
International Standard Book Number: 0-8092-5855-2

Published simultaneously in Canada by
Beaverbooks, Ltd.
150 Lesmill Road
Don Mills, Ontario M3B 2T5
Canada

Contents

Introduction

This is a book for people who want to keep their cars longer. Perhaps only a little longer, perhaps a lot longer. And, for some, beyond the foreseeable future.

Still, these car-keepers are not car buffs in the usual sense. Certainly they like the car they drive, but as for its mechanicals and innards, they are interested only up to a point.

That point seldom goes as far as tinkering with an engine or doing any maintenance more exacting than routine carkeeping. They are not do-it-yourselfers or Saturday Mechanics. Nor do they wish or aspire to be.

What they seek—perhaps as you likewise seek—is a strategy and an informed reason and way of doing things that, over the longest number of miles and years and at the least possible cost, will permit them to keep and drive their cars longer. And over these additional years and miles they want to find at reasonable cost the places and skilled craftsmen who can do the work that inevitably must be done to keep any car running well, safely, and economically—and as dependably as on the day its owner first took delivery.

Until this book there has been no guide for this kind of car-keeper. Perhaps the reason is that the conditions we are confronted with today never existed before. Now, for the first time, circumstances combine to give tens of millions of owners a variety of reasons for wanting to keep their cars longer than they have ever before kept a car.

These are today's new car-keepers.

It is to them—as to you, a newcomer to car-keeping—that this book is dedicated.

Part 1:
Car-Keeping Strategies

Chapter 1: Car-Keeping
Why It Makes Dollars and Sense

In the sacrosanct executive suites of automobile makers around the world, they call it the "wheeled revolution."

Who are the "revolutionaries"?

Virtually everyone who owns a car.

The ideology these millions of car owners turned "revolutionaries" hold in common has no parallel in history. It is an ideology that claims no political, religious, or nationalistic roots. Nor is it based on any of the timeworn doctrinal cornerstones. It is an ideology without written precepts or text, without a single soapbox orator or charismatic leader, without a guru or elder statesman. Neither can it claim even one representative in any world parliament, in any state assembly, or on the most obscure of county commissions. Despite its mass allegiance, and converts now numbering in the tens of millions, and though it undeniably holds the power to wreak economic chaos in the world's industrial nations, it is an ideology without a voice—and without a vote.

It is an ideology of almost simplistic, yet inordinately complex, decision. And it can be expressed (as in millions of households it is daily being expressed), in a single succinct sentence:

"I think I'll keep the car a few years longer."

It is a declaration of wheeled independence, the mark of a new genre of world-wide decision makers turned quiet revolutionaries: *the car-keepers.*

In all likelihood, you are one of them.

You *are* if you plan to keep your car longer than you have probably ever kept a car before—a year longer, two years, five years, a decade. Or, like some few, perhaps you intend never again, if you can avoid it, to buy another car.

As a car-keeper, you are a revolutionary in the wheeled revolution. You are a revolutionary because you no longer accede to—nor can you be motivationally coerced by—the long-cherished "buy words" (the decades-proven sales words) of the car makers.

As a car-keeper, you have rebelled against "psychological obsolescence," which once motivated most car owners to trade in and up every few years; against the "new model syndrome," which redefined *new* as *better;* against the "prestige factor," which imaged the automobile as the wheeled symbol of economic status and social prestige.

As a car-keeper, you have sent the motivational psychologists back to their couches.

More significantly, you and your car have become digits in the data banks whose out-tumbling graphs and forecasts are sobering the boardrooms of the auto makers and government economists every-

World champion car-keepers are London's cabbies. Many of their cabs, almost all of them diesel-engined, are still daily earning fares—after 20 years of stop-and-go driving.

where in the industrialized world.

What the graphs show—drawn from raw data which catalog every car-keeper's auto registration, model, year, and make—is that car owners by the multimillions are keeping their cars longer than they did a decade ago. And longer than the decade before that.

How much longer? The Roper Organization's annual poll of car owners recently found not only that the *overwhelming majority* of drivers plan to keep their cars longer, but also that nearly one-third (more than 30 percent) plan to keep them 10 years or more.

More conclusive for pollsters even than their own statistical findings was the unequivocal decisiveness of many car owners who said they planned to keep their cars far longer than they had ever kept a car before. The Roper poll's conclusion: Certainly, most of the new car-keepers were fully aware of what they were doing. And their decision was not only premeditated, but had been arrived at—as, likely, your own—only after long and considered thought. Their keep-it decision was not made pell-mell or offhandedly; nor was it a whim of the moment.

That the wheeled revolution, no happenchance, has been long coming, its momentum growing over the years, is documented in year-to-year car age data gathered by R. L. Polk & Co., the United States' premier chronicler of automotive trends.

Polk's figures show that today the average age of passenger cars on U.S. roads is nearing the seven-year mark—up from an average age of 5.5 years in 1970. Only during World War II, when auto production virtually ceased, and during the immediate postwar period, when automobiles were just again becoming available to a then eager car-buying public, did the average age of U.S. cars exceed the average age of those today. And the trend is indisputably an upward one.

Unfortunately the economists can take no comfort, as they did in the past, in the once certain knowledge that millions of longer-kept cars would ultimately reach the wear-out point forcing their owners once more into the showrooms. The reason lies in a whole bundle of parameters that make keeping a car longer—for a few years or for many—economically sensible, mechanically feasible, and socially acceptable.

Economically, today's new car-keepers are sophisticated nonbuyers. As car-keepers by choice, the majority, if they chose, could afford to buy new. But as calculating savers and spenders, they spend only if reasonably assured of appreciation (as an investment in a home) and shun what just as assuredly depreciates (an automobile). In their economic wisdom, they have chosen to keep fit what they now own and drive.

Mechanically, the highway's 55 mph national speed limit has stretched automotive wear-out into the distant future. Long past is the era of car-punishing marathon drives at 70, 80, 90 mph and higher. That era's demise has transfused years more life into nearly everyone's car. At an average of 55–60 mph, a well-kept engine is scarcely exerted. And its service life is significantly extended.

Socially, today's car-keepers find scant status in the undersized, underpowered, raucous-engined fuel economizers—fuel economizing itself being a fall from status—and far more in the cars, whatever their gas mileage, they now drive. By choice, they have adopted, over the automobile, a new cast of status symbols: a vacation to Europe, a condo, a cache of money-market certificates, a hot tub (and, for some, a live-in to go with it).

As car-keepers, they—as you—have rejected the long-foisted myths of the car makers.

Myth Number One: It is cheaper to buy a new car than to repair and keep the one you now own.

Hertz Corp., the car rental company that is among the world's largest buyers of automobiles, recently debunked *that* myth. From Hertz's own voluminous, computerized studies, a Hertz spokesman recently declared, "Under reasonably ordinary circumstances, it is Hertz's position that turning in an old car for a new one is *never* cheaper than keeping an old car longer. The cost of keeping the old car is less because depreciation is heavily front-loaded. Maintenance costs may go up, but they *never* approach the loss caused by depreciation. Moreover, insurance costs drop and interest is eliminated when the car is paid off."

Myth Number Two: Like anything mechanical, a car simply wears out.

A *car* never wears out—only its *parts* do. As they do, they can be replaced. Only a neglected car wears out—reaches the point of being economically beyond repair.

Vintage classic cars, as roadable today as the day sixty, even eighty years ago that they were manufactured, are but one proof that wear-out need never come.

Another was Mercedes-Benz of America's recent "Great Diesel Search." The object: to locate, if possible, the oldest and highest-mileage Mercedes-Benz diesel-engined cars still on American highways. High-mileage winner was a 21-year-old Mercedes-Benz 180D (the D for diesel), with 1,184,880 on its odometer, the equivalent of 100 years of normal driving.

Did its owner, Robert J. O'Reilly of Olympia, Washington, plan anytime soon to retire the car (even though Mercedes gifted him with a new diesel model)? Not at all. Declared O'Reilly, who was the car's fourth owner and had replaced its engine—reluctantly—at 750,000 miles, "I fully believe I'll be able to drive it another million miles."

Highest-mileage Mercedes-Benz discovered in recent "Great Diesel Search" had 1,184,880 miles on its odometer. Car-keeper Robert J. O'Reilly, Olympia, Washington, the 1957 180D's owner, said he expected to drive it another million miles—at least. (Photo courtesy of Mercedes-Benz of North America.)

Mileage runner-up in Mercedes-Benz's "Great Diesel Search" was a 1968 Mercedes-Benz 220D, with 912,000 miles—902,000 of them on its original engine. Its enthusiastic car-keeper is Edward Donaldson, of Eugene, Oregon. (Photo courtesy of Mercedes-Benz of North America.)

The top twenty high-mileage cars located by Mercedes-Benz had, in total, been driven 12,188,533 miles, or a bit more than 600,000 miles apiece.

Myth Number Three: When major components begin to need replacement—the engine, for one—it's time to get rid of the car.

Five decades ago that might have been true. Then, in depression year 1934, Cadillacs were priced as low as $2,395. Studebaker's prestigious President model was tagged $1,095 (if you picked it up at the factory). And you could drive a Dodge convertible coupe off any dealer's lot for about $800.

Inflation has changed all that.

Today, with virtually anything on wheels costing (with all costs figured) in the $7,000 and up—mostly up—range, even major replacements cost only a small fraction of the price for a comparable new car.

A new (remanufactured) engine, installed, seldom costs more than 10–12 percent of a new car's cost. Other major component replacements cost far less, percentage-wise, with a transmission rebuilding costing only 3–4 percent of a new car's price; a power steering unit replacement, 1½ percent; a front end rebuild 1½–3 percent.

But today's new car-keepers are not simply driving by the percentages. Nor out of fervor for cars, whether the one they own and drive or another. Neither, by any measure, would they call themselves revolutionaries. As for the wheeled revolution, they do not know, much less care, whether or not it even exists.

They are keeping their cars longer because keeping a car longer makes dollars and sense.

RISE OF THE 10-YEAR (OR LONGER) CAR-KEEPER

The Roper Organization's annual poll on automobiles and their owners is perhaps today's most inner-revealing car survey. Year-to-year, since 1973's OPEC oil embargo, it has been documenting an ever-accelerating trend toward car-keeping.

What the Roper poll shows is the following:

(1) An overwhelming majority of car owners now plan to keep their cars longer.
(2) Nearly one-third (more than 30 percent)* plan keeping their cars 10 years or longer.
(3) Car-keepers, whether they plan to hold on to

their cars only a few years longer or for as long as a decade or more, are fully aware of what they are doing.

Car-keepers candidly concede that their plan to keep their cars longer is, by the measure of earlier decades, unusual. As unusual, and new to many, as hanging on longer to their cars may be, they have joined the ever-growing ranks of car-keepers, though they may not label themselves as such.

Here, excerpted from the Roper poll, are some questions asked car owners—and the results.

- *Do you plan to keep your present car (the one you personally use the most) longer than you usually keep a car, or less time than you usually keep a car, or about the same length of time as usual?*

	1980 Sept./ Oct.	1979 Sept.	1978 Sept.	1977 Sept.	1976 Oct.	1975 Oct.	1974 Oct.
Longer than usual	64%	58%	57%	54%	56%	61%	59%
Less time than usual	4	4	5	4	4	2	2
About the same	27	34	32	35	34	31	32
Don't know	3	3	3	3	4	3	3

* projected through 1982

• *How long do you think you'll have your present car—that is, from the time you got it until you plan to get rid of it, how many years do you think you'll own it in total?*

(Asked of and based on those with car in family)

	1980 Sept./Oct.	1979 Sept.	1978 Sept.	1977 Sept.
1 year or less	2%	2%	3%	3%
2 years	5	7	6	7
3 years	8	10	8	9
4 years	8	9	10	10
5 years	14	14	17	14
6 years	10	9	9	10
7 years	6	7	6	7
8 years	7	6	6	6
9 years	2	2	3	2
10 years	30	28	25	21
Don't know	7	6	7	10

DEBUNKING RUNAWAY COSTS . . . AS A KEPT-CAR AGES

It is not true, as a continuing and fascinating series of studies by the *M*otor and *E*quipment *M*anufacturers *A*ssociation (MEMA) show, that a point is reached in age or miles where a kept car eats its keeper to poverty.

What is true, as MEMA's latest studies confirm, is what any car-keeper might suspect: as a car ages it needs more maintenance and more replacement parts. *But* the more is not checkbook unbalancing. Nor do these costs double or triple with a car's age. On the contrary, the average costs for replacement parts and service are not much different (or more than a few percentage points higher) after a kept car's 11th year than during its third to fourth year.

MEMA's studies and graphs (used here with special permission, and published under the continuing title "Car Maintenance in the USA") are derived from the largest data bank of its kind in the U.S., and likely the world. MEMA data are compiled through a quarterly, nationwide sampling of some 10,000 car owning households. While MEMA data*, to this point, do not wholly take into consideration so-called hard parts (major parts such as the transmission, engine,

* For additional and future data, contact: Director of Marketing Services, Motor and Equipment Manufacturers Association, 222 Cedar Lane, Teaneck, NJ 07666.

Fig. 1. *Undercar-ride products/services. Courtesy of the Motor and Equipment Manufacturers Association.)*

and gearing), the study comprises the car-keeper's most accurate insight into parts life expectancy.

In the latest of its studies, MEMA charts the usage rate and wear-out, by car age, of 33 automotive products—from Safety Products (brakes, lights, windshield wiper blades) to Cooling System Products (water pumps, thermostats, belts/hoses and antifreeze). The eight usage charts deserve close

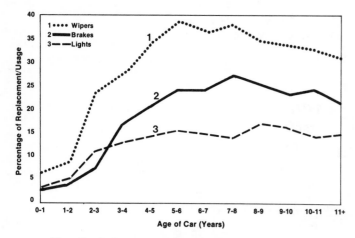

Fig. 2. *Safety products. (Courtesy of the Motor and Equipment Manufacturers Association.)*

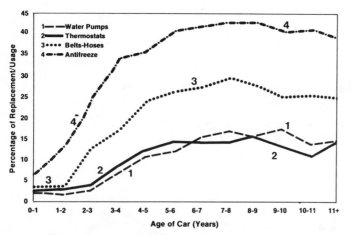

Fig. 3. *Cooling System Products. (Courtesy of the Motor and Equipment Manufacturers Association.)*

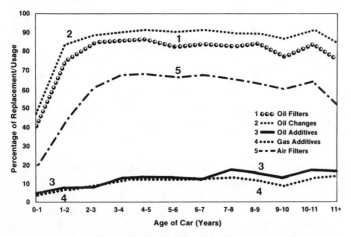

Fig. 4. *Additive-lubrication-filtration products. (Courtesy of the Motor and Equipment Manufacturers Association.)*

study. They document anticipated parts and product usage through any kept car's years and miles.

Here are some MEMA findings:

• **The rate of replacement usage dramatically increases (about doubles from what it was during the first year) as a car enters its fourth year.**

Cars zero to three years old (Fig. 8) account for less than 15 percent of total replacement parts and services. Cars four years and older account for the remaining 85 percent.

But from the fifth year on, parts usage remains virtually the same — give or take a percentage point — into old age, with cars 11-plus years actually using a fraction of a percentage point *fewer* parts than cars in the four to five year-old bracket.

• **As cars grow older, their owners neglect them more and more — when precisely the opposite should be true.**

Fig. 6 shows that cars are waxed far more frequently in their early years (the first three years) than later. The falloff of upkeep by car owners begins about the third year and continues downward, with some upturns, ever afterwards.

Owner neglect is also documented by Fig. 1, which shows that owners (obviously *not* car-keepers) tend to let tire balancing and front-end alignment go beginning somewhere after the fifth year, precisely the time when canny car-keepers strictly attend to Undercar Ride maintenance.

• **Some usage actually declines from its peaks with age.** Cooling system parts usage (Fig. 3) peaks between the eighth and ninth year and, except for thermostat replacement, actually declines a bit thereafter.

• **Seldom neglected, even by the most neglectful of car owners, are lubrication and filter replacement (Fig. 4).** These necessary-to-keep-it-running products and services remain in high usage throughout a car's life, as they must if a car is to have even average road life.

• **Overall, parts usage and replacement either rise only gradually over the years or (as in the case of appearance and ride accessories — as waxes and shock absorbers) actually fall off, due mainly to owner neglect.** This is dramatically shown in Fig. 7, which sums up all of the parts/service usage graphs. After the fourth or fifth year, parts usage and replacement rise modestly, if at all.

MEMA's computerized findings debunk the myth of car wear-out. While it is true, as every owner knows, that during its first few years (into its fourth year), a car uses fewer parts and services, once past the fourth year, replacement costs tend to remain, about the same (for the items surveyed by MEMA).

Despite what the myth makers would have you believe, there is no sudden, overwhelming time — whether in years or miles — when a car all but falls apart.

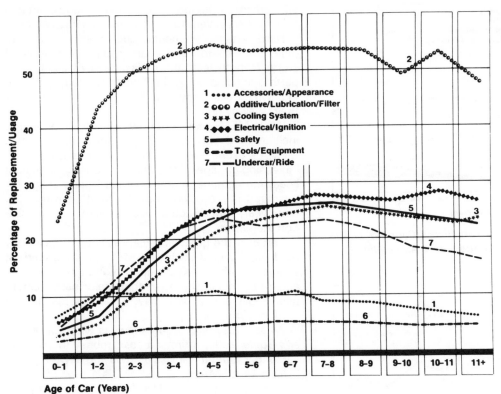

Fig. 7. *Average rate of replacement/usage for product groups. (Courtesy of the Motor and Equipment Manufacturers Association.)*

Fig. 8. *Distribution of replacement/usage. (Courtesy of the Motor and Equipment Manufacturers Association.)*

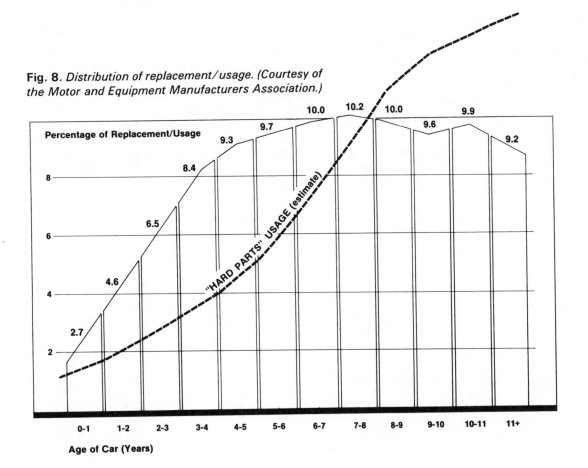

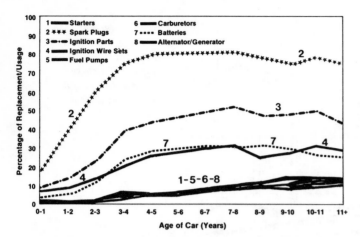

Fig. 5. *Electrical-ignition products. (Courtesy of the Motor and Equipment Manufacturers Association.)*

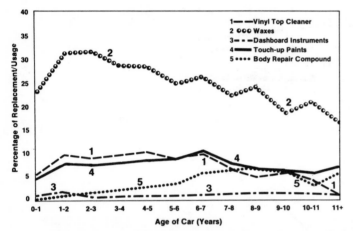

Fig. 6. *Accessories-appearance products. (Courtesy of the Motor and Equipment Manufacturers Association.)*

As shown in Fig. 8, cars three- to four-years-old consume some 8.4 percent of the total of all replacement parts, while a car 11-plus years old uses only

9.2 percent of the total — a full percentage point *less* than for cars seven- to eight-years-old (10.2 percent).

Hard parts replacement of such major items as engine, transmission and gearing may be a different story. Nonetheless, the replacement of costly hard parts is anticipated by this book's Strategy Scheduling, which also provides, amply in most cases, for their layaway financing.

While MEMA does not now, as earlier mentioned, include hard parts in its reckoning, Fig. 8 shows MEMA's *estimated* curve for hard parts usage with increasing car age. If this curve is correct, an almost linear (straightline) increase in hard parts usage (or overhaul) is predicted from the fourth through the ninth year, with an actual falloff of hard parts installation thereafter.

Certainly the greatest (steepest curved) usage for hard parts would seem, by MEMA's computerized estimate, to lie between the fifth and ninth years — again debunking the myth that major parts seldom need replacement until, say, a car has reached its ninth or 10th year.

What MEMA's charting shows is what *Car-Keeper's Guide* readily affirms: it costs money to keep any car longer, but far, far less than buying new.

Nor, as MEMA studies show, is a new car — or even a "young" car — free from upkeep and parts replacement.

In the automotive world, as in the real world, there's no free ride, and virtually no period in the life of any car, whether factory-new or a decade old, when maintenance and upkeep can be neglected. You pay for the cost of product replacement and service, except in a car's first year, and in rare cases its first two years, when the factory warranty picks up most replacement costs.

No one ever said that owning and driving a car was no-cost or scot-free — except by comparison: whatever the charted and anticipated costs of car keeping, they are modest compared to the cost of replacing the car you drive.

Chapter 2: Making the Keep-It/Trade-It Decision

It is seldom a snap decision. Rather, the decision comes gradually. You have decided—or think you have decided—to keep the car you now drive.

How long do you plan to keep it? Frankly, at that moment of final decision, chances are you don't know. Were someone to ask, you'd likely shrug, "Just longer—it all depends."

What the car-keeping decision most often depends on are a whole bundle of factors. In one way or another, these factors come together and add up to a keep-it decision.

You like the car and the way it drives. You like its looks, its lines and style, and the miles it gets to a gallon. While perhaps setting no EPA city or highway mileage records, its mileage is not all that bad. In fact, it's rather good. You see no reason to buy new simply for mileage—for the sake of 25 miles per gallon when the car you drive manages 20.

It is, moreover, a comfortable car—for you, its driver—and roomy for those who share its front seat or back. Its other pluses, the plus string now growing, may include its ability, without engine overstrain or depowering, to pull your boat or camping trailer, something today's small cars can't do or can only do with difficulty. Or, if a small car, it is roomier than most and manages even better mileage than most. Again, perhaps it is a neo-classic and

thus ageless in an aging kind of way—a car with pedigree, prestige, and milestone significance.

Gradually the pluses add up.

Economics may—as they have for many car-keepers—tip your decision toward keeping.

Assuming you can afford the average $9,500-plus for a showroom-new car, and would have no trouble, were you to finance it, in digging up the down payment, is a car—any car—really worth $9,500, $15,000, or $35,000? The latter figure is equal to a good hunk of house in some areas, a down payment on a spanking new condo in others. The same money, not spent for a new

Older, more powerful-engined cars easily pull the family trailer—one reason for keeping them. (Photo courtesy of Airstream Div. of Beatrice Foods Co.)

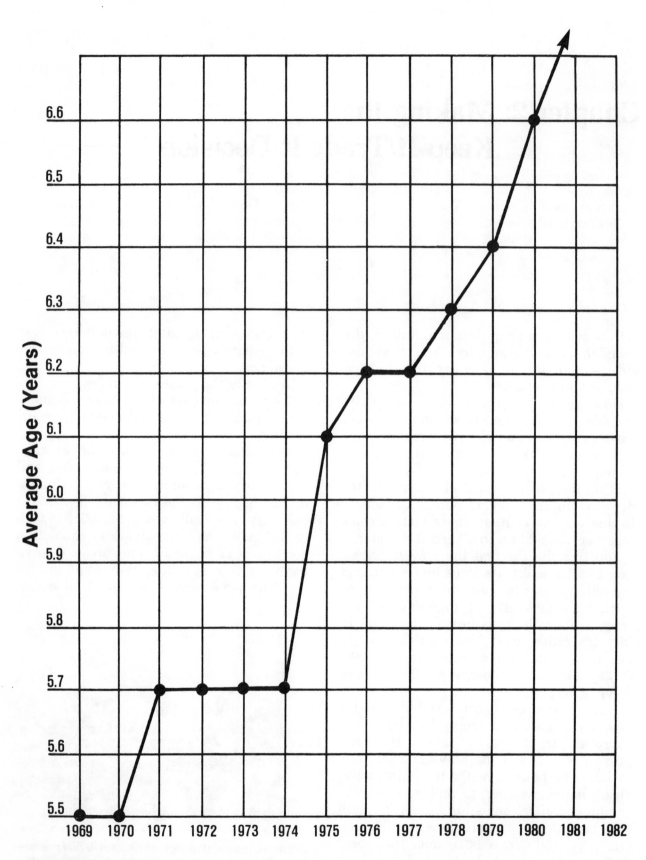

Average age of passenger cars in use in the United
States. (Data source: R. L. Polk and Co.)

car but invested in virtually any money account, might earn 10–15 percent, perhaps more, bolstering your income.

Money spent for a car, you reason correctly, is all outgo—and not simply the price of the car itself and its finance charges, but far worse, its almost as-you-watch depreciation. The biggest brunt of that depreciation falls in the very first year, when a new car's original value plummets by an average 30 percent.

Your doleful economic conclusion: buying new, now or in the foreseeable future, is next to nonsense.

But your perspective of yourself and the way others see you, as well as your image of your status and station among business associates and friends, may weigh even more heavily than all of the other factors combined.

Were you to keep the car, would you feel self-assured, even self-esteemed, driving it? Or would you forever feel somehow compelled to explain why it is not this year's model, or even last year's, or the preceding year's?

If you have long ago abandoned keeping up with the Joneses, who are keeping up with the Henrys, who are keeping up with the Browns—all of them having trouble keeping up with their creditors—you may smile to yourself and declare simply, "Enough of *that* treadmill."

So your thinking toward keeping turns more decisive. And it becomes even more so as you notice—and what car owner hasn't—that more and more drivers are keeping their cars.

Who, then, are the car-keepers? And how did they come to their keep-it decision?

They can be categorized and analyzed even as Detroit, with understandable consternation and no little haste, is belatedly doing so.

Car-keepers—by choice. By far the majority of car owners turned car-keepers, the voluntary keepers are yesterday's every-other-year buyers and, until just a few years ago, every three-or-four-year buyers, who now, both by choice and because of economics, want somehow to stretch still

further—perhaps to five to seven years—their car-buying interval.

Many among the by-choice keepers now view the automobile, as never before, as an unsound "investment." And, in fact, in financial terms it is a proven bad investment.

This is particularly true of those among the by-choice group who, unable or unwilling to pay cash, would expect to finance. They weigh the burden of financing a new car at today's 16 percent APR or higher. The same money spent not for a car but invested in virtually *anything* else—from pop art to popcorn futures—might *earn* the same percentage rate.

Moreover, having financed, the first-year depreciation (anywhere from 25 percent to 30 percent for most new cars) immediately reduces the worth of their investment by $2,500 to $3,000 for the average-priced car.

Were they to experience the same catastrophic loss in the stock market, they would cash in and get out. Rather than take an inevitable depreciation loss, they have taken themselves out of the car-buying market.

It is not difficult to understand why. In earlier years, a similar first year (front-end) depreciation, while almost identical percentage-wise, equated to a significantly smaller dollar loss. Thus a 30 percent first-year depreciation on yesteryear's $3,500 automobile cost the car buyer $1,050. The same loss percentage for today's $9,500–$10,000 model hands the buyer a $2,850–$3,000 loss.

And, while the no-win financial aspects of new car purchasing can be almost endlessly pursued—the traded-in older car has virtually no value; dealer profits, manufacturer-squeezed, no longer allow overvaluing of trade-ins or even a "good deal"—the no-buy mood of growing millions of by-choice car-keepers is based on a salient psychological shift as much as on down-the-drain economics. By-choice former new car buyers simply no longer view a new car as an object of prestige and status, nor as the symbol of the American Dream on wheels.

Many car-keepers by choice plan to keep their cars longer simply because they like the car and like the way it drives—as this 1980 Buick station wagon. (Photo courtesy of Buick Division, General Motors Corp.)

To the contrary, many have come to view a new car as a symbol of unsophisticated spending and of the susceptibility of its buyer (and driver) to the pitchman, whether he is on the showroom floor or on radio and TV.

Still, many among the car-keepers by choice want to keep their cars longer—often much longer—simply because they like the car they drive. If it is an older model, they appreciate its no-knock taste for lowest-priced regular and the uninhibited power of its antipollution-device-free engine.

These same by-choice car-keepers, in a surprising number of cases, believe the cars they drive (five to ten years old) to be better built than 1980s models, domestic or imported. Nor do they take kindly to the proposition of trading their roomy, powerful cars—able to seat six, able to pull a boat or trailer, able to tote home a roofload of do-it-yourself lumber—for the underpowered and undersized fuel economizers, domestic or foreign.

Many owners of recently made small cars, notably the imports, similarly like the cars they drive—their fuel economy, their long-lived styling—and, having paid more

for considerably less (a high price for their small cars), want to stretch out their investment by stretching their car's years of use.

For whatever reasons, and whatever the cars they now drive, these avowed car-keepers by choice—perhaps as many as 40–50 percent of all car owners—have decided to keep the cars they have for three to five years longer, for six to ten years longer, or for as long as they can.

Car-keepers—by necessity. Plain and simply—their numbers escalating as recession-inflation continues, and as new car prices relentlessly climb another 2–4 percent every calendar quarter—these new car-keepers are keepers with no other choice: they cannot afford to buy new. Faced with ever higher down payments, the value of their trade-in shrunk to near zero, their credit already stretched or nonexistent, theirs is a simple reality: keep alive what they drive.

Many among the car-keepers by necessity are newcomers to the ranks of turndowns: hopeful buyers rejected by lending agencies. Industry statistics show that 40–50 percent of new car prospects are nowadays turned down—for lack of credit.

Actually, the number is much larger since many who lack the means for obtaining credit have long since ceased being prospects—or visiting new car showrooms.

For necessity keepers, the choice is painfully clear: keep driving what they have or buy a used car. Yet many necessity keepers see no sense in buying used when what they drive is used. And, if nothing else, the car's frailties are known to its owner.

Financially, moreover, there is far more logic in spending $500–$1,000 or more to revitalize their owned cars than to buy used, only to spend as much or more to return it to some semblance of new-car roadability.

While the reasons the necessity keepers keep their cars differ from those of the by-choice car-keepers, their need is identical: to stretch out the useful life of the car they drive and, ideally, to return it, by incremental pay-as-you-drive corrective maintenance and rebuild, to like-new road fitness.

Car-keepers—forever. A still small but significant and ever-growing number of car-keepers do not plan, if they can avoid it, to buy another car ever again.

Two divergent categories of car owners comprise this group.

The first are the car-disgruntled, to whom a car is solely transportation. These owners view the whole process of car buying and dickering as game playing with their time and a tedium to their intelligence—and an economic rip-off, besides. While they may like the car they drive, they do not like cars in general. They put a car near the bottom of their "need to buy" list. And, if anything, they rate cars

much as does the dealer's salesman: as merely so much iron.

At some distant date these forever keepers might once again be persuaded to buy, but they would prefer never to buy another car, no matter what their present make or model.

Likely included in this group are a significant number of senior citizens who have a special attachment to their cars. Or, more profoundly, these people have decided to "drive out" their cars until the day, whether by choice or physical debility, they stop driving.

The second group among the keep-it-forever owners drive classic or neoclassic cars (vintage Ford Thunderbirds, for one example). Or they own classically crafted or expensive ultra prestige cars (as some Mercedes-Benz models)—cars that retain their status through the decades.

Nonetheless, keep-it-forever owners, as other car-keepers, share a common and increasingly urgent need: to make their cars last years longer.

Whether, having decided to join the car-keepers, you are a keeper by choice, by necessity, or a keeper forever, you are in good company—and a growing-by-the-millions crowd.

Other car-keepers by choice, having spent considerable amounts for their small cars, would like to amortize their investment over more years and miles than before. (Photo courtesy of Nissan Motors Corp.)

CAR-KEEPING QUIZ

Have you the temperament, patience, and persistence to be a self-assured and confident car-keeper? Not everyone has. Nor is every car owner psychologically attuned to keeping a car miles and perhaps years longer than ever before. This quick quiz should help you rate yourself as a prospective car-keeper.

	Yes	No
1. Little problems with your present car or, in fact, with anything mechanical you own, seldom bother you. You find out what needs fixing and in due time see that it's fixed.	☑	☐
2. You retain pride in ownership over long periods, whether it's your home, your car, or anything else whose purchase involved careful selection and a considerable financial outlay.	☑	☐
3. When a friend or neighbor buys a new car, you can't help feeling envious, even jealous.	☐	☑
4. You are not easily talked into having work done — around the house or on your car — until you have gotten more than one expert opinion as to whether the work really needs to be done.	☐	☐
5. You tend to act and think methodically. You are seldom panicked into costly, quick decisions.	☐	☐
6. You feel socially secure, whatever the occasion, as long as the car you arrive in, whatever its year or model, is well kept.	☑	☐
7. You rate the purchase of a new car as a costly, fast-depreciating luxury, and not as an investment.	☑	☐
8. The car you now drive, whatever its minor faults, is an old and trusted friend. You feel comfortable and secure behind its wheel.	☑	☐
9. When every fall's new models appear you rush to the car showrooms to see what's new.	☐	☑
10. You would not expect your living room furniture to be without a scratch after 10 years of use. Neither would you expect it of your 10-year-old car.	☑	☐
11. You know a few good mechanics you can trust. You would trust them to repair the car you now have and plan to keep longer.	☐	☑
12. You consider yourself conscientious in the routine upkeep of your car. You seldom skip or miss a regular and routine period for changing oil and filters and for having it lubed.	☐	☐
13. You are not convinced that today's new cars are "better built" or necessarily more economical over the long run than the car you now own.	☑	☐
14. You are acutely aware of how your car may affect your professional status. You would not be caught dead in your assigned company parking space with anything less than a late, luxurious model.	☐	☑

	Yes	No

15. Your family's second car — the one your wife drives — is older and less well kept than the one you drive. Driving *her* car always makes you feel a bit shabby and embarrassed. ☑ ☐

16. Even if you could pay cash for a new car today, you probably would choose instead to invest the money in money-market securities or in an interest-paying bank account. ☑ ☐

17. You are convinced that when one major problem crops up in a car it presages a rash of other major problems. At the first symptom of major trouble you usually get rid of the car. ☐ ☑

18. You are a woman alone. To you, your car is your fortress — a quick means of escape from any real or imagined marauder. But you are afraid — afraid that, as a car gets older, it may one day balk at starting, the key may fail in the ignition, or a door may be hard to open. Twice now you have dreamed those terrible dreams — and awakened screaming. ☑ ☐

19. Cars bore you. To you, a car is reliable transportation and nothing more. To keep your present car reliable, you expect — and are willing — to invest in necessary upkeep and repairs. ☐ ☑

20. Periodically you spray the interior of your now five-year-old car with "new car scent," purchased at any local auto supply store. ☐ ☑

Answers

While there are no pat answers to every quiz question, born-to-be car-keepers would have given these answers:

1. Yes	11. Yes
2. Yes	12. Yes
3. No	13. Yes
4. Yes	14. No
5. Yes	15. No
6. Yes	16. Yes
7. Yes	17. No
8. Yes	18. No
9. No	19. Yes
10. Yes	20. No

FRONT-END DEPRECIATION: EVERY CAR AN ECONOMIC LEMON

Since 1973 Hertz Corporation has annually issued cost-of-operation computer studies, based on its own 300,000-car rental/lease fleet — one of the largest operated by a single company. Based on these studies, Hertz concludes that longer ownership "normally lowers both cents-per-mile and dollars-per-year outlays . . . because the key depreciation expenses are almost always greater in an auto's early years."

This so-called front-end depreciation — a car's loss in value virtually the moment the buyer of a new car takes delivery — can amount, finds Hertz, to *nearly one-third of its purchase price during the very first year.* And, for all practical purposes, this depreciation takes place the moment it is driven, new, from the dealer's lot. While Hertz's computer studies show that the precise percentage of depreciation may vary widely from year to year, and often with make and model, "average depreciation rates," declares Hertz, "over an extended period . . . have been fairly consistent."

Hertz finds, on the average, that a new car loses 30 percent of its original value the first year; by its second, it is worth less than half its new cost; by its third year, it has lost nearly three-quarters of its value. And by the fourth year, it has lost more than 80 percent of its new cost. Here are Hertz's computerized findings:

FRONT-END DEPRECIATION

Year	Percentage of car's *original value* lost with succeeding years of use	"Book" or trade-in *value remaining.* Expressed as a percentage of car's original value
1	30	70
2	54	46
3	72	28
4	82	18
5	87	13
6	90	10
7	92	8
8	94	6
9	96	4
10	98	2

Chapter 3: Car-Keeping Strategy

If it weren't for the strategy involved, car-keeping wouldn't be as fun and challenging as it can be—or as easy on the car-keeper's budget as it often is.

The strategy of car-keeping is doing what has to be done but postponing what can be postponed. And whatever is done, moreover, is done according to a self-drawn *strategy schedule* based on a car-owner's average mileage. This schedule will:

1. *evaluate* a kept car's present condition and schedule work for the future;
2. *anticipate* major repairs based on the average mileage life of various major car components;
3. *assign priorities* according to whether the work is *postponable*, as an engine rebuild, or *nonpostponable*, such as safety-related work like relining the brakes or replacement of tires;
4. *budget* the shop-out of repairs pegged to a car-keeper's own car upkeep budget.

Sounds complicated? It isn't.

For starters, you already know approximately how many miles you usually drive each year—somewhere between 12,000 and 15,000, probably. You also know, because you know your car, what eventually has to be done to restore it to near-new condition if it isn't already nearly new. Likewise, you know roughly how much, each month, you now spend—and how much you can likely afford to budget—for car maintenance and updating.

All that's really involved in the strategy of car-keeping is putting it all down on paper as a guide. This also serves as a schedule that anticipates the wear-out of some components, the discretionary update of others, and the nonpostponable nature of still others.

Is car-keeping strategy, no matter how well charted and planned, infallible?

No, it is not.

Something may suddenly need attention miles earlier than might reasonably have been expected, based on average mileage wear-out experience. For one example, suppose the radiator suddenly turns leaky when, by mileage life expectancy and all odds, it should not have. Since fixing radiator leaks is nonpostponable, the radiator takes precedence over, say, the engine tune-up you'd budgeted for that month. A tune-up, desirable as it may be, is often postponable.

So everything on your strategy schedule gets shoved ahead—put off—a month. No matter; what really demands doing (the radiator) gets done. What doesn't (a tune-up) is postponed. And your budget isn't crimped or strained. This month the $50 you'd planned to spend on a tune-up goes to repair the radiator. Should the radiator repair come to $100 (in our hypothetical strategy financing, a two months' allotment of car-keeping budget), everything on the schedule gets pushed ahead *two* months.

And no harm is likely to be done.

But, you may shrug, anyone who owns a car *already* does that: has repaired what needs repairing and puts off what doesn't. That's true, but with one critical difference, a difference that goes to the very heart of what car-keeping is all about.

Car-keeping's carefully drawn strategy schedule ultimately aims at nothing less than the total *update* of a car and the *extension* of its life for miles and years. By contrast, the average nonkeeper—the car owner who does not plan to keep his car— hopes merely to keep it *running* until it is traded or sold.

Everything in the car-keeper's strategy schedule is concerned with keeping a car longer. It is scheduling built on *long-term* goals.

Precisely the opposite is true of the nonkeeper. He is concerned merely with maintaining the car well enough so that, come trade-in time, it retains some reasonable value. His goals are *short-term*. He does not anticipate, or even contemplate, major engine overhaul or major anything else. Were something major to crop up, he'd dump the car.

For this very reason, the non-keeper cannot justify more than a minimal investment in upkeep and repairs. He is, in effect—and from the day he takes delivery—"running out" the car until the day he runs back to the dealership to trade it in.

One of the reasons the nonkeeper finds a car so expensive over the short run is that, when forced to make a maintenance or upkeep investment, he seldom, if ever, keeps the car long enough to *amortize*—as do carkeepers—that investment over a number of miles and years.

Suppose the nonkeeper is a four-year trader. He trades at four years or 60,000 miles, whichever comes sooner. He does this because he knows—has been told— that after the fourth year maintenance expenses are sure to be higher than during a car's earlier years.

But, as so often happens, he might be forced during the third year to install a new water pump, buy new tires all around, take the car in for its third brake relining, and have the power steering pump replaced. Within six months he trades in. In so doing, he loses virtually every penny of his considerable maintenance investment.

The dealer pays him not a cent for "good rubber"; rather, the car's trade-in value would go down if the tires were bad. Nor does the owner recoup a penny for the power steering and water pumps. And he doesn't pocket a dime for the $150 he spent, less than 6,000 miles before, on the brakes.

In the automotive game, the nonkeeper is a sure *loser*.

Car-keepers, playing the same game, are all sure *winners*.

Every nickel the car-keeper puts into repairs, routine maintenance, or updating is driven out to its full worth and value. And then some.

Car-keepers, who recognize their can'tlose status in the car game, seldom wince at replacing a water pump. Not at all. They know, by all odds, that it should carry them through another four years, maintenance-free. The same applies to tires, to the add-on of a vinyl top, to a sunroof. Amortize their cost over the kept car's lifespan, and whatever the cost, it is piddling.

Consider that vinyl top. Let's say it costs $100 installed. And let's suppose you drive

In car-keeping strategy, bias-ply tire costs are often easier to fit into your strategy budget. But the radial tires have longer tread life because the tire cords run almost perpendicularly across the tire and the belts run around the tire's circumference, restricting tread movement and thus improving tread life. The bias-type tire uses cords run diagonally, thus the name bias, *which results in often significantly shorter tread life than for the radial—but the bias tires cost far less. (Drawing courtesy of the Tire Industry Safety Council.)*

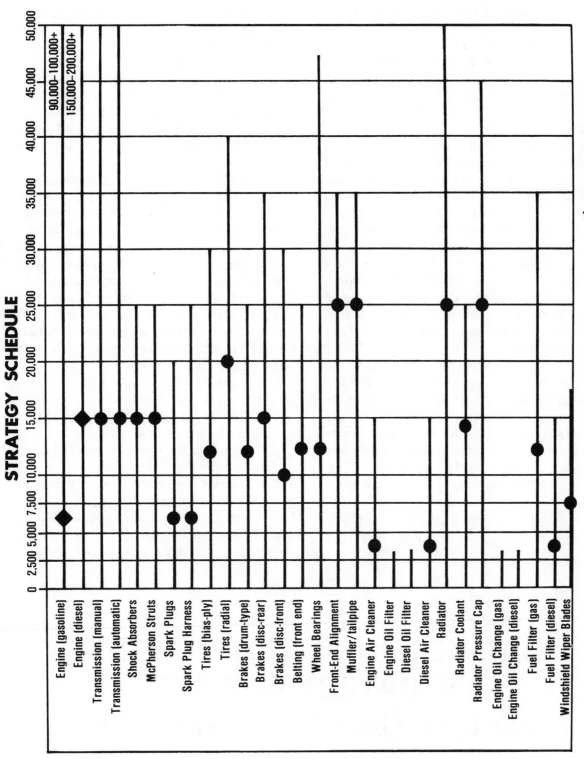

your kept car another 10 years. The top has cost you $10 a year. But for the nonkeeper the economics are all wrong. Install a vinyl top in the second year on a car to be traded in four, and the top costs $50 a year—an expense hard to justify.

Thus, in the strategy of car-keeping, virtually any expense within reason, when amortized over a car's extra years, can be justified. And more: costs very little over the long run.

Therein lies the basic and critical difference between work a car-keeper may elect to have done or to postpone and the same do-it/postpone-it decision of the nonkeeper. It explains, moreover, why nonkeepers are sure losers in the car game and why car-keepers are sure winners.

For car-keepers, everything eventually gets fixed and some things get updated. Even so, if averages hold, you should end up spending no more per month—during any month—than your monthly strategy budget provides.

And, while car-keeping strategy sets no monthly budget amount—whether $25 (unrealistically low) or $150 (certainly more than most keepers would anticipate budgeting)—a realistic $100 a month seems to get more done more quickly with less strain on most budgets. (See box, "Car-Keeping's $100 Monthly Strategy Budget," below).

That $100 is far less than the nonkeeper, financing his short-term car, pays merely in depreciation and finance charges each month. Besides, even though you may budget $100 a month in your car-keeping strategy, nobody says you actually have to spend it or even lay it away in a special strategy bank account (although, wisely, some car-keepers do).

It works this way:

Looking over your strategy schedule, you may decide—or a mechanic may decide for you—that something, maybe replacement of front-end belting, can be put off another few months. So you put if off and spend nothing.

In fairness to car-keeping strategy, however, the money—real or on paper—is still in your strategy account. And here's why it should be. Come a really major job—transmission or valve work or repainting—you'll have to forgo months enough, at $100 a month, let's say, to be able to shop out the job when, on paper or in hard cash, you've accumulated the cost of the work. This could mean putting some little things off for six months or more to pay for the necessary bigger thing.

Car-keeping by scheduled strategy doesn't nickel-and-dime you to death. Rather, again using our hypothetical figure, it may $100-a-month you to death.

But you end up the sole owner (with no finance company co-owners) of a fit-as-factory-new car—free of monthly payments save for what you've strategy-budgeted for car-keeping—and with a kept car that, over its life and miles, should prove the least expensive car you have ever owned.

CAR-KEEPING'S $100 MONTHLY STRATEGY BUDGET
Far Less Than Non-keepers Pay

Buying new, the driver who does *not* intend to keep a car for more than four years spends an average *$168.88* monthly for maintenance, tires, financing, and depreciation — contrasted to the *$100* monthly strategy budget many car-keepers find adequate for maintaining and updating their kept cars.

The $168.88 monthly the nonkeeper pays is derived from a breakdown, by car accountants Runzheimer and Co., of average national costs for operating and maintaining a car.

In the accounting below, Runzheimer, perhaps the leading U.S. authority on car costs, based its study on a 1981 Chevrolet six-cylinder (229 cu. in.) Malibu Classic four-door sedan with standard accessories, including power steering, automatic transmission, power disc brakes, and radio, but not air conditioning — a car driven 15,000 miles a year using unleaded gasoline at an average cost of $1.30 per gallon.

Variable Costs	Average Cost Per Mile
Gasoline (unleaded) and oil	6.27¢
Maintenance	1.18¢
Tires	.72¢
	8.17¢

Fixed Costs	Annual Cost
Comprehensive insurance ($100 deductible)	$ 76.00
$250 deductible collision insurance	180.00
Property damage and liability insurance ($100,000 bodily injury for one person/ $300,000 bodily injury for more than one person/ $50,000 property damage)	254.00
License, registration, taxes	88.00
Depreciation	1,287.00
Finance charge (20% down; loan @ 15%/4 yrs.)	490.00
	$2,375.00

With these national average figures in hand, let's see what the nonkeeper either pays or loses, the latter being eventual money out of pocket, to operate a car.

Straight off, the nonkeeper is hit by two annual big-ticket costs: $1,287 in depreciation and $490 in finance charges. Neither of these big-bill operating costs accrues to the average kept car. First, by its fourth and fifth year, a kept car will have already lost some 85 percent of its original value through depreciation. (See box, ''Front-End Depreciation: Every Car an Economic Lemon,'' page 18). Second, the average four- to five-year-old car, if financed, has been paid off and is free and clear.

Tire costs for both, however, are the same: 15,000 miles x .72¢ per mile = $108.00. The nonkeeper's maintenance costs will be *less* — 15,000 miles x 1.18¢ = $141.00. The very reason for the $100-a-month strategy budget is in anticipation of higher kept-car maintenance costs.

So, let's add up the nonkeeper's annual costs, divide them by 12, and see what, other than for insurance, fuel, and licensing, the nonkeeper pays monthly to operate and maintain a car.

Annually

Depreciation	$1,287.00
Finance charges	490.00
Maintenance	141.60
Tires	108.00
	$2,026.60 *per year*

Monthly

$2,026.60 divided by 12 = $168.88 *per month*

The car-keeper's realistic $100 monthly strategy budget for maintenance and updating is very considerably less than the average $168.88 the nonkeeper pays. Nonetheless, it should, in all but rare instances, amply cover the costs in the strategy of keeping a car longer.

SETTING UP YOUR OWN STRATEGY SCHEDULE

Setting up a strategy schedule isn't difficult. The doing is a onetime thing. Do it once, and it should last the life of your car.

While you can use the strategy schedule sample shown in this chapter, yours will be far simpler. The sample has listings for many items your car doesn't have. Yours will be considerably shorter, too.

So, while you can use the book's chart, you really should make your own, based on your car and on the miles *you* drive. Just once, put it down on paper — which is all setting up a strategy schedule involves — and you'll have it for all times.

Your starting point for scheduling what has to be done routinely in car-keeping is the present reading on your dashboard odometer, which records the number of miles your car has been driven. Unless you are beginning car-keeping with a brand new car, your odometer will certainly read something other than zero or near zero.

But, except for some long-range items — items that usually don't have to be attended to until thousands of miles down the road — you can start your strategy schedule at zero. You can do so, however, only if, at the outset, you have a few things done to start you right in car-keeping. And, for the majority of car-keeping items, these things will permit you to treat whatever your odometer reads as zero.

The things you should have done to allow you to consider the odometer's reading as zero, and also to make things simple, are things any car could probably use, anyway. So, do these things: Have the engine tuned. Have the oil changed and a new lube oil filter installed. Have the air cleaner changed, something that is usually done during the tune-up, anyway. Have the brakes inspected so you know about how many miles more they can go without overhaul. And have a tire man estimate the residual tread miles that remain before you'll need new tires. Do these few things, and you can start car-keeping, starting your strategy schedule at zero for most items.

This is because you have, at the start, taken care of most of the things that have short mileage maintenance intervals. Having been done, their schedules — as the strategy schedule itself — start at zero.

For some other items — the longer-ranged ones — you'll have to mark strategy lines to take into account the obvious fact that their scheduled checking will not fall at the mileages shown in the example schedule. They won't because you have already driven a goodly number of miles. And those miles have to be accounted for in the scheduling.

Let's take one example: automatic transmission servicing, scheduled to be done at least every 15,000 miles. Suppose your car's odometer reads 12,000 miles. You have that many miles on the car and that many miles on the automatic transmission.

Even though the strategy schedule calls for automatic transmission servicing at 15,000 miles, for you and your car, servicing of the transmission actually lies just 3,000 miles — not 15,000 — down the road. This kind of thing will occur in the scheduling of all long-range strategy items, since you are already, say, 12,000 miles along the way toward having them attended to.

Adjusting your strategy schedule to take into account what your odometer reads is easy. First, whatever the odometer's reading, round it off to a logical and convenient figure. Suppose it reads 12,234 miles, Call it 12,000 miles. Second, subtract this already-driven mileage from the strategy mileage on each long-range item's strategy line.

Thus, with an automatic transmission servicing due at 15,000 miles, you would subtract the 12,000 miles the odometer shows from the scheduled 15,000-mile transmission servicing — and get 3,000 miles. That's when transmission servicing is scheduled.

On the automatic transmission's strategy line you mark an X at 3,000 miles. And, continuing along the line, mark another X every 15,000 miles more. Now that particular item's strategy has been adjusted to the miles you've already driven and to what your odometer reads.

It's as easily done as that. Do the same thing for *each* long-mileage item on the strategy schedule, and the entire car-keeping routine starts at zero — at the starting line of the strategy schedule and, in effect, at the starting line for making any car last years longer.

You've not only adjusted the strategy schedule to account for the mileage you have already driven, but you have, in a few minutes' time, created a strategy schedule that precisely fits your car and its to-date mileage.

Every month you need only check the odometer's reading, each time subtracting the mileage it read at the start, to know precisely where you are along any long-mileage item's strategy line.

Let's say that a month from the day you start scheduled car-keeping the odometer reads 13,300 miles. Since you started with it reading 12,000 miles, you subtract the starting reading and wind up with 1,300 miles. This is the mileage driven for the month.

Glancing at your strategy schedule, you can see immediately what, if anything, needs doing. At only 1,300 miles probably nothing on the schedule will need doing. But next month, with perhaps 2,500 miles accumulated from your car-keeping starting point, there will be things that should be done or are close to needing to be done.

The author — who has used a strategy schedule for years — pastes a little label next to the odometer. The label shows the odometer reading when the author began strategy scheduling. Doing that, there's no chance of forgetting where the odometer was — and what it read — at the start.

And so you have begun what is really your car's second life — its strategy scheduled life.

Another useful thing to have in car-keeping is a permanent record file of every itemized bill for every nickel's worth of maintenance done on the car. Such a simple record file — a loose-leaf notebook is all you need — becomes a quick reference in strategy scheduling. And an extremely valuable one.

First, you have readily at hand, and all in one place, a record of everything done. Billings usually show when maintenance was done because mechanics invariably read your odometer when they write up a work order and note the reading on the order. Should a mechanic fail to do this, make sure that you do. That way you know, for every increment of maintenance, what was done, who did it, and when, by calendar date and odometer reading, it was done.

Besides the billings, your loose-leaf file is also the place to keep any warranties you receive — for tires, battery, shock absorbers, and mufflers, typically.

Those warranties represent car-keeping dollars you don't have to spend. So, too, may those itemized work orders and their billings.

With the warranties ever ready, should something go wrong with a warranted item, you can often have the item replaced at no cost to you, simply because you have kept and can show the warranty. This also makes obvious the fact that the item failed while still covered by warranty.

If the battery is warranted for 36 months but goes dead in 18 months, you pay only a prorated amount for a new battery, deducting for the months remaining in the battery's warranted life. For a 36-month battery that died in 18, you would probably get a new battery at around half the price the dealer is quoting for new. But to do it, you need to have that warranty in hand in most cases. File it in your loose-leaf strategy file, and you'll have it when you need it.

A loose-leaf file also becomes positive proof to a mechanic who may have forgotten, or chooses to forget, that he did a job and precisely when he did it.

Suppose you had a power steering pump unit installed and three months later it failed. Its work order and billing, there in your loose-leaf file, become the kind of evidence few shops or mechanics can ignore. Very likely the shop will install another steering unit, charging you only minimal labor or perhaps none at all. And very probably you will not be charged for the pump, since it, in turn, is warranted to the mechanic by the pump's supplier. He merely returns the pump to his supplier, who credits the mechanic's account. But without the shop's original work order and billing as proof that the shop did the work, you are not dealing from strength.

Keeping every work order and billing involved in strategy scheduling may come in handy, too, at income tax time, providing you can take some or all of the car's expenses as deductions.

As for setting up the strategy schedule, at the very outset of car-keeping you might need to spend half an hour — an hour at most — on this task. And that, insofar as scheduling is concerned, is your total time investment for the life of your car.

It can be the most profitable — and money-saving — half hour you ever invested.

CAR-KEEPING FOR PROFIT

While most car-keepers want only to keep and drive their cars longer, some kept cars are what big-time auto auctioneer Rick Cole dubs *milestone cars:* post–World War II models, which may be more popular among car buffs today than when new. A good milestone — meaning not only the right car but one kept in near-showroom condition — may be worth several to ten times its original cost.

Among the milestones most in demand, thus demanding at resale far more than their new cost, are all of the Ford Mustangs of the mid-'60s, with the convertibles and coupes leading the Mustang worth-more pack; almost any of the once teen-favored "muscle cars" of late '60s and early '70s vintage (they were knocked out by OPEC's 1973 oil embargo): the Plymouth Road Runner, 455 Pontiac Trans Am; the Carroll Shelby Ford Cobra GT-500, a modified Mustang, and others of their street muscle (meaning high-performance cars designed to perform that way on city streets rather than on a track).

Add, too, such milestones as the MGs (MGA and MGB models), the V-8 engined Triumph TR8 and even Detroit's historic design disaster, the short-lived 1958-59 Ford Edsel, currently restored to favor by car buffs and car buyers.

Other cars of the post–World War II era worth keeping are the traditional "worth more" models and name brands — Mercedes-Benz, some Cadillacs, and likewise some Lincoln Continentals, among them the 1957 Mark II, plus some imports.

Although nearly all of the milestones are worth more than when new, some are worth many times their original showroom sticker price. In 1981, a 1966 Ford Mustang convertible, fully restored and in showroom-new condition, brought $21,000 at auction in Tulsa, Oklahoma. New, it had cost $2,650.

None of these are true classics, or anything like them. A *classic,* by the Classic Car Club of America's definition, must have been built before 1949. Even so, a classic is not a classic unless officially recognized as such by the Classic Car Club.

Still, the postwar milestones are definitely worth keeping. Your investment in upkeep is very likely to be recouped, at least, should you decide to sell.

Advises auto auctioneer Cole, "The key to making money in cars is hanging on." Hanging on is certainly one reason for keeping a car, but not, for most who keep their cars longer, the only reason.

BUYING USED FOR KEEPING

Does it make sense to buy a used car with the intent of keeping it? Some car-keepers believe it does, and for a number of reasons:

• They dislike the car they now drive, yet don't want (or can't afford) to buy new. But they do have in mind a particular make or model. If they were to buy that model used, they'd certainly plan to keep it, something they don't plan to do with their present car.

• They are temporarily without a car, due to a wipeout accident or serious mechanical trouble. They need wheels *now* — and as inexpensively as possible, which in all probability means buying used. Whatever used car they buy, they'd want to hang on to it.

• They are inveterate used-car buyers who normally keep their used cars as long as practicable.

• As parents of a first-car son or daughter, or as searchers for a family around-town second car, they prefer, faced with today's high new car costs, to buy used now rather than wait until they can afford to buy new later. They, or their kids, always put a lot of miles and years on any car, new or used.

Where, then, can you find and buy a good used "keeper car"?

Owner surveys taken by the author, confirmed by nationwide studies, show that (1) there *are* good used cars to be had; (2) they can be purchased, even on today's market, for considerably less (30–50 percent less) than buying new, and (3) they can be bought with considerable assuredness — in some cases, backed by warranties — that they are, indeed, "good used cars." As such, they would be good buys for the prospective car-keeper.

Some sources of good used cars are obvious. Some are not. Here are three good sources for potentially good used cars:

• *A friend, relative, or neighbor,* whose car and car-care habits you know. That person should (1) average fewer than about 12,000 miles annually on a new car, (2) drive conservatively and carefully, (3) be a bug for having maintenance done when it's supposed to be done, and (4) be an early trader, seldom keeping a new car more than two to four years.

• *A "glitter" used car lot* is another source. And this is *not* to be confused with the usual used-car lot.

Explains John C., who has bought several good used cars from the "glitter" lots: "Shopping for a good used house, you'd logically expect to find it in a neighborhood where people can afford to keep up their homes and do. Same applies to cars."

John C. shops at only the most glittering of the glitter lots — the used car lots of new car dealers in the swankiest, most expensive parts of town or, as often, in the even more posh, better-heeled suburbs.

Doing so, he often finds himself in the company of the wealthy. There is one difference. *They* are buying new cars. *He* is buying *their* used cars.

Virtually every car shown on a glitter lot is a "cream puff." Most of the carriage-trade new car agencies unload (wholesale to volume dealers) fully 50–70 percent of their trade-ins, cars that simply don't meet their own high standards for "used." What's left — on some lots, fewer than 20–30 cars — are usually the best used cars in town — and often for miles around.

"We can't kennel dogs," a glitter lot manager shrugs. Why not? Because, in the main, the dealership's used-car customers are the same well-heeled clients who also buy its new cars. Shopping for a used car, they look for — and demand — quality. But not necessarily because they expect to drive the car themselves. Most glitter lot cars sold to the same dealership's new-car clientele are second, third or fourth family cars, intended for a teenager or, as often, for a housekeeper or relative.

Glitter lots are indisputably high-toned (but not necessarily high-priced) mavericks in the used-car trade. Most do not sell on Sunday, nor lavishly advertise or otherwise hawk their wares. Many even shirk the word *used.* On the glitter lots you'll find signs advertising "Resale Cars" or "Previously Owned Vehicles."

"Hardly Used" might be more fitting, considering the mint condition of many of the pampered, late-model, low-mileage cars usually stocked by the glitter lots.

A recent visit to a glitter lot (in an area of $200,000-plus homes) showed this:

Eight of the 11 "previously owned" cars for sale that particular day were "house cars" — cars originally purchased off the dealership's own sales floor. Five of these wore door stickers documenting that they had been regularly and solely serviced in the agency's own shop. And three, originally lease-purchased (the way those in lofty tax brackets prefer to buy), were still under full-maintenance contracts to the dealership. All 11 were one-owner cars, anywhere from two to three years younger than the usual used car. And, with one exception, their odometers showed extremely low mileage for their age.

Concludes John C., "It's not who you know, but *where you go* to buy that counts, when you're shopping for a really good used car to keep."

• *Used lots of the major car-renters* —Hertz, Avis, National, and Budget — are a third source. These are probably the very last places you'd expect to find a good used car. But they are actually among the first places to look for a good, keepable used car.

For the moment, put out of mind all the "no-good-

Buying used to keep? Some of best used cars—and only ones with good as gold warranties—are often found on used lots of major car rental companies.

nik'' things you've heard or read about rental cars: that the average rental machine, in its 12- to 18-month rental lifespan, is handled — or mishandled — by an average of 83 different drivers; that people too often rent to drive where they deign not to drive their own cars (into all but roadless wildernesses, on local hot rod courses, or on skid-prone winter trips); that the average renter never checks under the hood, and, if he did, couldn't care less. It's not his car or, mechanically (other than for collision damage), his responsibility.

All of these things are true up to a point. Executives of the big rental companies admit it. But only a tiny fraction of their thousands of rental cars are ever maltreated by their renters and drivers.

Among rental cars, there are also some that are the bona fide best of the lot. These are the ones the big rental companies hold back and sell on their own lots. The major rental companies offer more than simply top-grade used cars. They offer what no other seller of a used car — not your great aunt, not the average used car dealer, and not even a glitter lot — comes even close to offering: fully warranted, mechanically documented used cars.

The major rental companies hand you (1) a maintained machine meticulously, mechanically kept by the book (or even better); (2) a car warranted by the rental company for the first 12 months/12,000 miles, at least, and in some cases, for as long as 24 months /24,000 miles; (3) a car with an often mile-by-mile, computerized service and repair record, usually yours to inspect — a rare pedigree for any used car.

Rental *resales* — the term the rental companies use for their rental fleet trade-ins — are the *only* used cars readily obtainable with a documented life history, assured professional maintenance, and a good-as-gold warranty. What's more — again unlike virtually any used car source you can name — most of the rental used car lots encourage your taking the car you intend to buy to your own mechanic for a third-party appraisal.

How good are the rental used car warranties? Consider just one among dozens of used rental-car buyers surveyed from coast to coast by the author.

Nancy C., of Miami, Florida, bought a two-year-old car from the local Avis agency — a car with far more miles (nearly 60,000) than the average (23,000 miles) for up-for-sale rentals. Nonetheless, the car came with Avis's 12-month/12,000-mile warranty. With only one month remaining on the warranty, Nancy's Avis overheated and conked out on a Miami causeway. She had the car towed to a garage, rather than back to Avis, a mistake she now admits to. The garage "tore the engine apart," she says, and arrived at a verdict: a cracked engine block.

Only then did Nancy C. phone Avis, who, as within its rights, responded that it could hardly be expected to warrant an engine now in pieces — and one its own mechanics had not seen. But, on considered second thought, Avis agreed to abide by its warranty, even in the warranty's final month. What Avis put into Nancy's car wasn't at all what she had expected. Avis installed a *brand-new engine.*

Because the major rental companies warrant their used cars, they cannot afford to keep, or to sell as used, a car in anything less than fit condition. They wholesale to local used-car dealers most of their fleet — cars not up to their rental-lot standards. Most of the big rental outfits abide by the "$500 Rule": any car whose repairs, during its rental life, have exceeded $500 (not much in today's repair market) is automatically wholesaled.

Given even the best of the rental fleet cars, there is at least one secret to finding and buying the best of these rental best. It lies in a single salient rental statistic: 85 percent of car renters are business people. Most are airport renters: they pick up a car at a rental agency's airport location, drive it on local business calls, and return it to the same airport location.

Wholly unlike the maverick rental few who rent to drag race or swamp hunt, these vast majority of business renters treat their rentals precisely as they treat their personal cars at home. They are notably cautious, conservative drivers. And they rent, for the most part, conservative but sometimes luxury-appointed cars — again, much like their own personal cars. The cars they rent, which in time become the big rental agencies' best used cars, are dubbed by some rental experts *easy mileage* cars. Whatever their mileage, it adds up to easy — well-driven — miles.

In shopping the rental lots for a good used car, shun the sports car, the flamboyants, and others of their ilk. Select a conservative car (a car no rental hotfooter would set boots in), and chances are the car you buy will be an easy mileage, strictly-for-business car, driven all of its rental life by careful and conservative drivers.

Any major rental agency's conservative-model used cars can be as good as any good used cars available anywhere today.

Chapter 4: Born-Again Oldie
Showroom-New at One-Third the Price

Buying new, as millions of owners of older cars (cars nudging five to eight years) are deciding, isn't necessarily buying better. Still, does it really make dollars and sense to *rebuild* a car?

My answer—and decision—was yes. I decided to have rebuilt, front-end to tail-pipe, my then eleven-model-year-old 1968 Dodge Coronet 440, a one-owner oldie (I had purchased the car new).

Precisely as should you, as should any prospective car-keeper, I carefully weighed the pros and cons of my dump-it/rebuild-it decision.

Author's born-again 1968 rebuilt and customized Dodge Coronet, now with nearly 200,000 miles on its odometer.

I liked the car. I liked the way it drove, the way it handled, and responded. It was an old and trusted friend. We had come more than a few miles and years together. And I liked its then midsize. (I say "then," because by today's sizing it is a big car.) Precisely because it was mid-size, it was roomy and comfortable, with none of the backseat (and even front compartment) leg-cramping common to today's minimodels, midsize to compact.

Moreover, I liked the car's lines and good looks, as I had the day, nearly eleven years before, that I'd taken delivery.

Still, though gifted with good, even sporty lines (made sportier in the rebuild

by some easy add-ons: new wheel covers, a vinyl halftop, and a luggage rack on the rear deck), it was—and is—no classic among cars. Nor, I knew, was it ever likely to be. In its showroom-new days it had never been the most popular car on any block. Indisputably, however, it had proven itself road reliable—in fact, remarkably so.

Save for every six-months routine tune-ups, its 318-cubic-inch V8 engine (judged by many experts as among the most sturdily dependable power plants ever churned out by Chrysler) had lived, by any reckoning, to an astounding old age. It had managed 157,496 honest miles with only average car care. And not once, in all those miles, had its innards been touched, much less tinkered with.

Statistically, my Dodge's engine had lived the proverbial nine lives—and at least 50,000 miles longer than does the average gasoline V8. And, while it was no longer going strong (it gulped a full quart of heavyweight oil every 250–300 miles), it was going. And it probably would continue to run for at least another 10,000–20,000 miles. Perhaps even longer.

My ultimate decision to rebuild was, in part, a calculated experiment in car-keeping. I hoped, in the doing—more precisely, in the *having done*, for I intended to shop out all of the work—to be able to answer, with the jaundiced insight of one who has been there and back, the myriad questions confronting those who face the same keep-it/dump-it decision. This book grew largely out of that experiment.

It was, in its way and in its time, a pioneering research—and eventually it would be cover-acknowledged as such in an issue of *Motor Trend* magazine.

Certainly others before me had rebuilt their cars. Few, if any, however, had set out with a single avowed intent: to document—in text, statistics, and photos—the rebuild of a plain jane among cars.

Nor, likely, had any before me documented as carefully the psychological and fiscal traumas—the vexations of shopping for the right mechanics at the right price,

the days without wheels while my rebuild was in one shop or another, and the costs, down to the last bolt and washer.

As research into the practicability of car-keeping, my rebuild was unique not so much for what it was as for what it was not. It was *not* the backyard-common do-it-yourself rebuild.

Unlike most rebuilders before me, I almost totally shopped out the mechanical tasks. In other words, I had virtually all of the work done by others—mechanics, body menders, electrical specialists, pin-stripers, and painters.

I shopped out the doing because the majority of today's new car-keepers—you are probably among them—are *not* do-it-yourselfers. Nor have they, or you, either the wish or the mechanical savvy to be. Nor could they spare the considerable time required to do the work themselves. Neither, in all truth, could I.

Bluntly, few among today's first-time car-keepers hanker to tear into an engine, strip a transmission to its gearing, or tinker a radiator to rights. *That* is for the back-shop do-it-yourselfer and car buff, which the majority of today's car-keepers are not.

But shopping out the work admittedly complicates the economics. Unlike do-it-yourselfers, most of today's new millions of car-keepers must rebuild at "retail": pay the not inconsiderable price of having professionals do the rebuilding for them.

One key question I intended to answer, in rebuilding my Dodge "at retail," was whether, at today's high labor costs, to say nothing of parts costs, rebuilding would prove economically feasible.

Do-it-yourself rebuilders reckon their own labor at zero dollars and cents. Certainly, they may shop out some engine machining. But doing most of the work themselves, they face no "retail labor" outlay. And many, besides, buy the bulk of their rebuild parts from discount part suppliers or even pick them up used, relatively cheap, from auto junkyards.

Car-keepers turned car rebuilders can, of course, buy some discount parts, even from junkyards. But probably the majority of car-keeper rebuilders have neither the time nor the desire to peruse the parts houses, new or used. They will, by convenience and choice, buy at "retail."

When you shop out the rebuiding "at retail," you pay not only the full cost of whatever the mechanic is asking for his labor, but also the full cost—and often a substantial markup as well—for the parts the mechanic installs.

Shopping out the rebuild is, most certainly, not accomplished on the cheap.

Purposely, also, I had chosen to rebuild—as may many car-keepers—a plainly average model: a bench- (not bucket-) seated, two-door sedan without air conditioning, FM stereo, or most other luxury amenities, though air conditioning and a stereo 8-track tape deck were added during the rebuild. All things considered, the Dodge was an average midsize for its day and even in its day, except for its designed-in good looks, a plain jane.

Moreover, my selection of one of yesteryear's plainly average models (rather than the same-vintage but near neoclassic Corvette, Buick GS-400, or Continental Mark III) aimed, bluntly and perhaps finally, to answer the return-on-investment part of the rebuild question. Namely, in today's market (or, for that matter, in any day's market) does it make economic sense to rebuild? Can you—were you to sell—recoup all or most of your rebuild investment?

Eight months, $2,452.79, and half a dozen mechanics, tinkerers, and body-righters later, I had the answers to that and other questions most often asked by those who plan to keep and eventually to rebuild their cars.

The rebuild bill (see itemized accounting, "Costs of Rebuilding," page 35) was a bit more than *half* the showroom-new cost of the car in its vintage 1968 year, but only about *one-third* the cost of a comparable new car in the year it was rebuilt (1978) and likely only *one-fourth* the cost of a similar car today.

Considering even escalating parts and labor costs, as a rule of thumb a car-keeper

Author's 1968 oldie needed almost total bodywork— not unusual when properly rebuilding a kept car

First of several coats of enamel—in original factory color—covers primer coat which hid extensive bodywork and paint make-ready.

should be able to have rebuilt an 8- to 10-year-old car for roughly 25–33 percent of the cost of buying a comparable new car in whatever year the rebuild is done.

But the rebuild and its costs need not be confined to a few months, or even necessarily to one or two years. The doing and its costs can be spread out over two to three years, so as scarcely to make a dent in even the best-balanced budgets.

My own rebuild accounting is, by any

Essential for protecting any paint job are rub strips, here being installed on author's car during its rebuilding. Rubber or vinyl strips fit into aluminum channels installed along car's sides.

reckoning, somewhat inflated—the cost of rebuild being *less* than the itemized total. My itemized total, for example, includes *all* rebuild costs. Included are nearly $300 worth of items that, more rightly, should be *deducted* as normal costs of maintenance and upkeep. Replacement of tires all around ($162.58), is one example. Every car owner expects to replace tires in the normal course of ownership. Replacement rubber is not properly a rebuild item. Neither is the relining of brakes (in the rebuild's case, only the front brakes required work)—a $76.60 item that is also a normal car-use, not rebuild, expense. Routine radiator repair ($45) can be expected every three to four years under normal and usual driving conditions, depending on where the car is driven and how dutifully its owner maintains its rust-inhibiting antifreeze coolant. These and other maintenance items and their costs were included because they were part of the total cost of rebuilding the car to showroom-new appearance, performance, and safety.

If these normal maintenance items, plus some others that obviously have to do with maintaining the rebuild's good looks (wash and polish, chrome polish, etc.) are tallied, and their approximate $300 sum deducted

from the total, the bottom line cost for rebuilding my Dodge stands more accurately at *$2,150.*

Undeniably, as did I, you will include in the rebuilding more than a few items of a strictly normal maintenance nature, because they represent money actually spent.

So let's return to the out-of-pocket rebuild total: $2,452.79. What the money bought was stem-to-stern bodywork and repainting ($613.85); a front-end rebuild and alignment, plus necessary brake work ($248); automatic transmission and torque converter rebuild ($247.50); radiator reconditioning ($45); new tubeless F-78-14 whitewall tires all around ($162.58); and the go-withal to make it all work—a remanufactured identical-to-new 318-cubic-inch V8 Dodge engine ($912.44 installed).

With the basics looked to, I added—as do most who rebuild—some goodies to update the car's looks, or more properly to customize it: a vinyl halftop ($85), gold vinyl striping ($35), and a rear-deck luggage rack ($79.45).

From a junkyard I picked up a set of factory-original stainless steel wheelcovers ($32). And, I had installed maroon scuff-moldings ($45), matched to the Dodge's original and retained same color. The moldings, running along both sides of the car, protected the new paint job and added a racy flare. Another $3 spent for new license plates in California's then new blue color, replacing the age-dating former black and gold plates, helped visually to shave away the years.

For my money I got a customized reconditioning with even better than original good looks—that, and some answers to questions every car-keeper asks:

Can my car be rebuilt to look like new?

Yes. Nearly any car can be. But the more poignant question, perhaps, is "Once it's rebuilt to look like new, will I be proud to drive it?"

If you expect your rebuilt car to look like this year's models—or next year's—you'll be disappointed. But if, as many owners of older cars (whether two model years old or

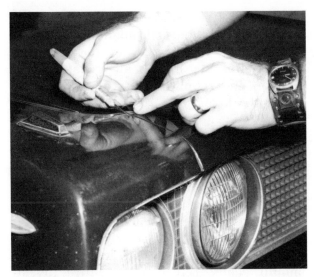

Professional vinyl striping added finishing customized touch to author's rebuilt car. Only a striping pro can do the striping job right.

Rear luggage rack goes on, as the rebuild nears completion. As a contributor to rebuild's styling, the same $80 cost of rack was a bargain.

ten), you liked the car then and like it now, chances are you'll like it even more once it's rebuilt.

Is rebuilding really worth the time and trouble?

That's for you to decide. Rebuilding my Dodge Coronet consumed hours of searching out parts, finding the just right (and right-priced) specialists to handle each job, a chore that included a 200-mile round trip drive and an overnight stay in a distant city motel while the old engine was being hauled out and the remanufactured new one installed (a transplant, incidentally, that took a mechanic and his helper the better part of eight hours).

The time and trouble, however, size down to minor inconveniences if you do the job *piecemeal*, over weeks, months, even years, rather than all at once.

Are there cars that shouldn't be rebuilt?

Definitely. Rebuilding has but a single purpose: to restore or retain a car's *like-new* condition. Rebuilding, by definition, makes the basic assumption that the car is *structurally* sound to begin with and that what's wrong is merely *mechanical*, which includes normal bodywork.

Car-keeping is *not* wreck-keeping.

Auto insurance adjusters are among the most astute judges as to whether a collision-damaged car is keepable, and thus repairable. Often, against the protest of its owner, an adjuster will declare a wrecked car "totaled," and thereby tag it for the scrap heap. The reason is simple: the adjuster knows that the cost of repairs—of rebuilding the car to its original

Remanufactured engine is lowered into author's car during its rebuilding. Engine was identical to old one. Engine switch took mechanic eight hours.

condition—will exceed the value of the car. *Even more important, he knows that no amount of rebuilding will return it to its structural like-new condition.*

Rebuilt, will it drive and handle like new?

Drive, track, and handle like new (or close to it), yes. But *ride* like new—like a five- to ten-year younger model? That depends.

If you do a lot of things right—install new tires all around (four new ones, not just one or two), have new shocks installed, and are careful to have the front end aligned and to have the tires and wheels precision balanced—then there is no reason why it should not ride as it did when new. For that's how it came from the factory—with new tires, new shocks, balanced tires and wheels, and a factory aligned front end.

Restore those and you'll restore its ride.

Can I expect to be finished with repair costs once it's rebuilt?

No, of course not!

Operate any car—brand new, rebuilt, or in between—and you expect routinely to spend money for repairs. Rebuilding doesn't change any of the normal expenses of operating an automobile, though once it's in near- or like-new condition, you probably will find yourself spending less for some things—oil, fuel, and the like. But basic car costs and basic repairs don't change, and rebuilding certainly does not eliminate them.

Once it's rebuilt, can I expect—should I sell—to get my rebuild investment back?

That depends on the car you rebuild. Rebuild some neoclassics and you may wind up selling for $10,000 against a rebuild investment of $2,500.

More normally, in today's market, a $2,500 rebuild—just to pick a figure—should easily return your entire investment, come time to sell. But it also depends on to whom you sell.

A used car dealer, going only by his used-price book, might offer a few hundred dollars, while a car buff would gladly pay all that you invested in the car and very probably considerably more.

But certainly most car-keepers don't rebuild to sell. They rebuild to keep—to keep and drive a car longer, likely, than they have ever kept or driven a car before.

They are car-*keepers.*

And so, of course, am I. That is why I had my car rebuilt, why I still happily drive it, and why I expect to be driving it into the foreseeable future.

COSTS OF REBUILDING

Itemized and subtotaled are the costs of rebuilding the author's born again 1968 Coronet 440 Dodge. While your costs will vary (add 20-25 percent to update these 1978 figures), shown are the parts, materials, and labor that typically go into almost total rebuilding. Even if you were to add 30 percent to this bill, the total — about $3,200 — is likely to be less than one-third the price of a comparable new car.

ENGINE		Subtotals
Remanufactured complete engine: V8 318 cu. in. Dodge (plus $115 refunded core charge)	$643.00	
Engine accessories		
Carburetor, 2 barrel, rebuilt exchange (plus $16 refunded core charge)	28.98	
Spark plugs, 8	5.04	
Ignition wiring (harness)	8.00	
Motor mounts (2 @ $4.00)	8.00	
Oil pressure sensor valve/switch	1.69	
Radiator hoses (2), top and bottom	6.58	
Radiator hose clamps (2)	1.38	
Dipstick tube	2.25	
Radiator cap for closed circulation system	1.75	
Air filter	1.79	
Oil filter	2.79	
Oil, 5 quarts break-in SAE 30	5.75	
Antifreeze coolant, 2 gallons	6.14	
Engine paint, 2 spray cans	4.30	
		$727.44
Installation: remove old engine, install and tune new	$185.00	
Total engine costs:		$912.44

TRANSMISSION		
Transmission and torque converter rebuild (includes removal, rebuild, fluid, and adjust)	$247.50	
Total engine and drive train:		$1,159.94

BODY WORK (Repair, Repainting, Striping)		
Body work and complete repainting (original color)	$466.75	
Rear left fender light	6.04	
Trim molding for 3 wheel wells	32.86	
Panel, rear underdeck	17.60	
Turn indicator, right front fender	10.60	
Molding, antiscuff, car length both sides (material and installation)	45.00	
Striping (material and application)	35.00	
Door trim, plastic	.78	
Total repaint and body work:		$613.85

RADIATOR		
Radiator, repair and replace	$ 45.00	
Total radiator:		$45.00

FRONT END AND BRAKES

Front end rebuild: parts, labor, alignment		$200.00
Parts included in price:		
Upper control arm bushing (4)	$17.08	
Idler arm assembly	21.79	
Lower ball joint assembly	33.22	
Upper ball joint assembly	33.22	
	$105.31	
Brake reline and align wheels		48.00
(only front brakes required relining)		
Parts included in price:		
Brake linings (1 set)	$21.00	
Wheel cylinder kits (2)	5.60	
Brake fluid	2.00	
	$28.60	
	Total front end and brakes:	$248.00

TIRES AND WHEELS

Tires, 4 new F-78-14 wide tubeless, poly glass-belted 4-ply (actual) polyester cord/2-ply fiberglass, whitewall: mounted and spin-balanced (retained steel valve stems)	$162.58
Wheel, spare wheel (replacing damaged), from wrecking yard	6.00
Wheelcovers (OEM), used from wrecking yard, $8.00 each	32.00
Total tires, wheels, covers:	$200.58

APPEARANCE ITEMS (major, exterior)

Vinyl halftop	$85.00
Luggage rack	79.45
Total appearance items:	$164.45

MISCELLANEOUS

License plates, new (Calif.)	$ 3.00
Polish, for chrome	.89
Wash and polish	13.50
Steering wheel cover	2.98
Lubrication (lube only)	3.58
Total miscellaneous:	$20.97
TOTAL REBUILDING COSTS:	**$2,452.79**

Chapter 5: The Mechanic Connection
How to Get It Done Right for the Right Price

He is persuasively reassuring. So is the sign in front of his shop that proclaims his membership in one of the better associations of his trade. With certain confidence, he extends a coveralled arm beneath your car's hood. Seemingly as practiced as your family physician, he takes the pulse of his patient: your engine's carburetor.

A *good* mechanic, you tell yourself in self-congratulations at your own good luck.

He may be no such thing. Rather, he may be among the significant percentage of auto mechanics (some experts put the figure at 25 percent—one out of every four) recently branded by congressional investigators as "grossly incompetent." So incompetent, in fact, that eight out of ten shops asked to check an undercover car planted with a simple mechanical fault either wrongly diagnosed the trouble (and repaired something else) or couldn't diagnose or repair it at all.

Even if he *is* a good mechanic, he may not be good for you, the car-keeper.

Testimony before another consumer-oriented congressional committee showed that 29 percent of every repair dollar spent goes for "unnecessary repairs." Whether correct or not, and the figure has since been challenged, it does not even consider charges made for work not done, parts never installed, labor not expended, and other frauds perpetrated by mechanics on the driving and car-keeping public.

Small wonder that of all consumer complaints auto repairs have for years ranked number one.

Despite the apparent ripe pickings for almost anyone with a tire tool or torque wrench, a number of 1980s factors make finding a mechanic—good, bad, or so-so—harder perhaps than ever before.

Over the last decade some 56,000 service stations and new car agencies have quite literally closed up shop—shops once staffed by mechanics. Then, too, fewer youths are opting for mechanic careers. And not only has the United States wheeled population grown by 30 million vehicles since 1970, but people are keeping what they drive longer—which calls for repairs.

To make the bad worse, underhood is proliferating a new generation of electronic gadgetry, from minicomputers to electronic ignitions. Almost all of it beyond the knowledge of the average mechanic and certainly far beyond the traditional tools of his trade. Nowadays, it takes an electronic analyzer (costing as much as $20,000), a kind of computer itself, to savvy auto electronics.

Thus has evolved the *replacer*, and not simply for electronic repairs. He replaces parts (a time-saver for the shop, a bill-raiser for you) rather than repair them. In some shops a single good mechanic rides herd on half a dozen replacers. He tells them what to replace, a quick old-for-new exchange that demands minimal mechanical know-how.

When a shop proudly presents you, along with its bill, a handful of removed parts as proof that the work was really done, often the "work"—as once defined—wasn't done at all. What should have been easily repaired at modest cost has been replaced at immodest cost.

If, to this point, you have concluded that the car-keeper can't find a good mechanic, take hope. You can. In fact, you can find something ever rarer: the supermechanic, the totally knowledgeable specialist in whatever you suspect is wrong with your kept car.

To do so takes time. It requires getting recommendations from friends, other mechanics not specializing in the work you want done, or your auto club. And it may take experimentation; a recommended shop may not prove as capable as touted.

Over the years, and no different than any other car-keeper, I have found five supermechanics: one specializes in brakes and front-end repair and alignment; another, in automatic transmissions; a third in the radiator and its cooling system; a fourth in matters electrical and electronic; and the fifth, in more general repairs, including the engine.

With one exception (the general and engine shop, which has a dozen employees), all are small operations, the owner being the chief mechanic. None advertise. All are out-of-the-way places. All are independents (not franchised). And all, though they would waive the rule in any car emergency, are by-appointment-only places (in marked contrast to the harried, hurry-up drive-in-anytime shops).

At these independent, low-rent-district, by-appointment shops you are on a driver-to-mechanic basis. You can discuss what needs to be done directly with the mechanic who will do the work.

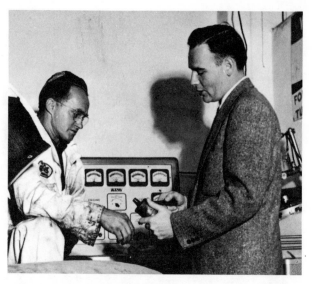

In a small, independent super shop, you can talk with the mechanic (likely its owner) who will do the work. In many large shops you can't.

At many other shops you cannot do this. In fact, at most dealerships, big garages, and franchised operations, you are not *permitted* to talk with the mechanic. Instead, you work through an intermediary—the estimator or order writer, who in turn usually works on commission, earning more the more he writes on your work order. Bluntly, he is nothing less and nothing more than a salesman. What he is selling are parts and labor. Typically, the shop earns 60 percent of every labor dollar (and hour) the estimator writes up and 40 percent on every part—down to the smallest bolt—it installs. The estimator takes a commission on the total. And you pay for them all.

The small supermechanic places you'll find don't figure that way at all. First, they're not burdened with high rent and a salaried superstructure of executives, estimators, cashiers, and yard men (go-fers who fetch cars and parts). Moreover, the small shop mechanic can bill you only 50 percent of the $25–$40 hourly labor rate charged by the big operators—and still take home more pay than the big operators' own mechanics. So, right off, you may save 50 percent in labor costs, which often form the bulk of any car repair.

While the small supermechanic places do

add a percentage for parts, they tend to add less and to install fewer parts. No executive, as at the dealerships and franchise places, scans the small mechanic's every work order, demanding to know why more parts weren't installed.

Besides, the small independent super shops I found—as can you—stand 100 percent behind their work. There is simply no argument. If the work is wrong—and it rarely is—it is righted.

In such shops, whose owner-mechanic knows his customers by name, you and your kept car are important customers because you are important to the mechanic. In the bigger shops, particularly the dealerships, your business counts very little. There is always another car and its distraught owner driving through the door.

The small super shop has other advantages. For one, you are seldom, if ever, hit with a "five o'clock surprise"—a monstrous add-on of work you didn't authorize or expect, which you discover at 5:00 P.M., when you pick up the car.

At a small super shop you *know*, going in, what the costs will be—and sometimes, to your amazement, the final bill is *less* than you had agreed upon or expected.

If unknowns plague a job—as they often can—the small mechanic, once he sets to work, calls to explain that he has found something he thinks should be fixed. In the big shops you are seldom called. When you are, you can be certain that it is bad news, not good. Bad for your bank account, good for the shop's.

I have had my super brake mechanic call with *good* news: the wheel drum on the brake job he was doing didn't need machine turning, after all, reducing the job estimate by $30.

Do such things ever happen in the big places? Perhaps as often as about every fifth eclipse of the moon. And the worst among them are the big dealerships. (I am thinking of a certain large local dealer shop . . . but then, I would rather not. And neither would you.)

Equally important, the supermechanic takes the time to explain what's wrong,

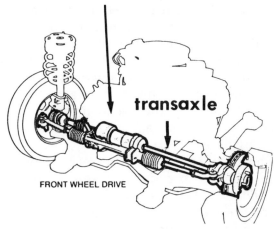

Front-wheel drive repairs may cost more than similar repairs on cars rear-wheel driven. In a front-engined, front-wheel drive car, everything is upfront with the engine—including the drive axle and transmission. Components are harder to reach and to work on. To repair a part, many other parts may first have to be removed, which takes the mechanic's time and costs you money.

what isn't, and what's involved. He may even suggest what work can be put off to accommodate adjustments in your strategy schedule. Over the years he takes special interest in your kept car, even if only because you've decided to keep it and he has a role in that plan.

As for finding supermechanics where you live and drive, they are there, if you take the time to look.

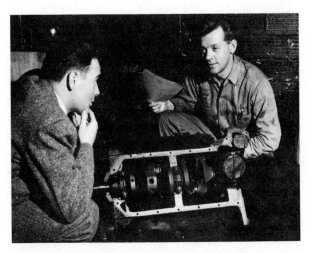

A supermechanic takes the time to explain what's wrong and the alternatives you may have if major engine work is involved.

Until you find them, it may be worth knowing—if you are a member of either an American or Canadian automobile club— about the clubs' fast-spreading net of "certified" shops and garages. These places are carefully club-screened, and they agree to abide, in case of disputes between you and the mechanic, by the decision of the clubs themselves, which act as sole arbiters in such disputes.

The certified shops must meet stringent requirements in order to retain their club certification: (1) They must offer a written work estimate, which may not be exceeded by more than 10 percent unless specifically authorized by you. (2) They must hold available, for your inspection or the club's, any replaced parts. (3) They must warrant the repair for 90 days or 4,000 miles. (4) They must employ mechanics certified as competent in their specialty by various of the mechanic-certifying organizations.

The American Automobile Association (AAA) and its affiliate clubs call theirs the American Authorized Repair Service (AARS). More than 1,250 shops and garages, most of them independents, are AAA certified under the program in 22 states and the District of Columbia. Your local AAA office will send you a list of AARS-certified shops in your area. But the AAA will not arbitrate a dispute unless you are a club member.

The Canadian Automobile Club (CAC), which was first with the certified shop concept, now certifies some 1,200 repair places in all Canadian provinces and territories.

What, though, of the small super shop's prices? Can you expect a job estimate by its owner-mechanic to be cut-rate? The answer is yes and no. No, because he is a specialist and entitled, good work that he does, to a specialist's wage for his work. Yes, because not only is his job estimate habitually lower than those of the bigger, high-overhead, rush places, but he springs no surprises—no add-ons, no ups, no games. And he is invariably honest. If he thinks your kept car needs a new fan belt, there is little question that it's needed.

Make mechanic connections like these, as you can, wherever you drive and live, and you'll get the work done right—and priced right, too.

Part 2:
Car-Keeper of the Century:
Louie Mattar

Louie Mattar is not your usual car-keeper. Unlike most readers of this book, he is a professional do-it-yourselfer. And much more: an automotive innovator. Few readers would aspire to be either. Yet all of us are inspired by living legends. In the world of car-keeping, Louie Mattar is one of those legends.

Nowhere in all the world is there a car that equals the white 1947 Cadillac sedan, now with nearly 470,000 miles on its odometer. Nor is there a car-keeper anywhere the likes of the Cadillac's owner, 71-year-old Louie Mattar.

Together, by Mattar's own reckoning, they have five times been featured in *Popular Science,* twice in *Life,* five times more in *Popular Mechanics,* and in countless other magazines and newspapers around the world. In 1952 Louie and his kept car made the first of a record fourteen appearances on "You Asked for It," a top TV show of the '50s. That first appearance drew 20,000 letters from viewers who couldn't believe their eyes—or TV screens. In the years since, Mattar and his showroom-new but now more than 35-year-old Cadillac have

appeared on other TV shows, including "Mission Impossible" and, in 1981, "That's Incredible."

Louie Mattar's car *is* incredible—as is Louie himself, a self-taught former electrical engineer at Ford and General Motors and a wizard mechanic's mechanic. Over the years Mattar has spent numberless hours, inventive genius, and more than $75,000 to create the century's most ingenious and utilitarian kept car. Twentieth Century-Fox, the motion picture company, once offered Mattar $100,000 for the car, which he says is today worth closer to $1 million.

But Louie Mattar isn't selling. Nor would you, if your car—as Mattar's—were installed with such nonfactory amenities as a shower (hot and cold water), a medicine cabinet, a bar, a drinking fountain, an electric washing machine, an ironing board, a coffee maker, a refrigerator, an electric

This 1947 Cadillac's backseat has all the built-in conveniences of home—including electric washing machine, electric range, refrigerator, toilet, sink, TV, ironing board, coffee maker, and virtually anything else you can imagine. (Photo courtesy of David Covey.)

"Car-keeper of the century," Louie Mattar refreshes under 1947 Cadillac's built-in shower. On-the-move tire changing mechanism is seen hydraulically extended here. Car can also automatically change its own oil. (Photo courtesy of David Covey.)

range, fold-down beds, a sink, a toilet, a TV, a two-way radio, and a telephone. But these are simply homey frills, installed mainly to please Mattar's wife, Rose.

What pleases Louie—and astounds the best engineers in automotives—is considerably more. The Cadillac can drive *nonstop* from Los Angeles to New York City and back (6,320 miles round trip) and did so in 1952. Two years later it wheeled *nonstop* the whole 7,482-mile distance between Anchorage, Alaska, and Mexico City, arriving

in the Mexican capital precisely one minute ahead of the time scheduled on Louie's rigorously kept timetable.

If your car and mine can't accomplish such nonstop road feats, it is because they are not designed to change a flat tire while doing 50 miles an hour on an expressway; at the same speed to inflate a tire that's loosing air; with the flick of a dashboard switch, to change its own oil; through an elaborate electronic self-surveillance network, to constantly monitor every pulse of its own engine and its accessories.

Louie's Cadillac can.

It can, likewise on the move, change its own fuel pump (should the old one fail) as well as the ignition system's critical condenser and coil. And it can switch to any of three sets of brakes—hydraulic (the car-common type), vacuum, and air, the latter more common to trucks. Just as easily, it can switch from one battery to another (it has four big marine batteries, the high-energy type used in submarines).

It's just as unlikely that your car is a mobile service station.

Louie's is. It tanks more than 230 gallons of gasoline, 15 gallons of oil, and reservoirs 30 gallons of water—some of this, admittedly, trailered behind the car.

And it can be fueled on the move—by tank trucks which, at prearranged spots along the highway, draw alongside, at Louie's radioed bidding, to fuel by special transfer hoses. Or it can be fueled by helicopter.

The car is also an on-the-move self-service station. A phalanx of electric pumps can flush dirty oil from the engine's crankcase (even as new oil is automatically added), flush the toilet, and supply the car's shower, wet bar, drinking fountain, and sink.

"Sometimes," recalls Louie, now retired and living with his wife (and *the* car) in San Diego, California, "I'd spend months just figuring out how to do something. Most of what I did, you know, had never been attempted before—or since."

RV Magazine once called Louie the grandfather of the recreational vehicle, noting that his Cadillac had all the comforts of today's motor home in the days when RVs were sternly utilitarian. Long before RVs generally came to rule the recreational roads Mattar and his wife—and their recreational Cadillac—were camping in automated comfort.

But automotive challenge, more than recreation, spurred Louie Mattar, during off-hours (he owned a garage) and weekends to customize his kept car beyond imagination—and, say some, almost beyond all reason.

How, you might ponder, does one invent a system for changing a car's tire while driving? Push one of the more than 75 switches on the Cadillac's instrument panel—it is far too gadgeted to be called merely a dashboard—and the "how" becomes audibly and visibly evident.

From somewhere hidden beneath the car there is the hiss of hydraulics—as an equally concealed 10-ton hydraulic jack lowers, from its fold-up undercar position, one of four spare wheels—to pinch-hit, until it is changed, for the one with the flat. Louis flips another switch and, with more hydraulic hum, a working platform slides out from nowhere. Its purpose is to give the tire changer (the job must be done physically, from outside the car) a platform on which to stand and work. But armed as an assistant (necessary for tire changing) is with an electric impact wrench, its 110 volts supplied from an on-board power generator set, the changing comes off smoothly. And though Louie slows to safe changing speed, the job is done quickly.

Obviously, if one has in mind to drive nonstop—precisely what Louie had in mind when designing on-the-move tire changing—there can be no stopping. Not for flats, not for an oil change, not for a tune-up—all of them, one way or another, totally automated in the Mattar Cadillac.

Perhaps the ultimate test of Louie Mattar's nonstop inventive genius is the car's method of inflating its own tires while they are rolling. Involved is a complex system of high-pressure air lines running in passages drilled through the axles. Air is supplied—you guessed it—from an on-board compressor. The compressor can also be activated to blow air continuously over the tires to cool them. And somewhere hidden from sight are, in total, 13 separate starting motors to get all of Mattar's automation going.

If anything, the Cadillac's tuned-to-perfection 200-hp engine—a mere 50 hp above its original power—seems commonplace among so much that is uncommon. But Louie assures that the engine is no such thing: valves, pistons, and other parts were all specially made.

All of these add-ons, built-ins, and hidden-aways have boosted the car's weight to 8,500 pounds, nearly twice its showroom weight. To compensate, Louie

It takes two to "fly" Mattar's now world-famous car, its dashboard set with more than 75 switches, lights, meters and gauges. Codriver monitors the blinking, flicking, alarm-sounding works. (Photo courtesy of David Covey.)

designed special springing and added those extra air and vacuum braking systems. The car, never a fuel miser, is even less one today.

Nowadays, the car-keeper of the century and his automotive marvel only occasionally cruise the highway. And seldom, anymore, on the kind of nonstop drives that once made headlines and caused TV viewers around the world to doubt their eyes.

The problem is not Louie Mattar's 71 years. He is in robust good health. The problem is finding a copilot (merely a co-

driver would scarcely do) to handle all those instrument panel switches and gauges. The car that knows no equal performs best with two in its cockpit.

Obviously, there are simply too many gadgets, switches, gauges, and monitoring lights for a driver, alone, to keep his eyes on, and still keep an eye on the road.

Part 3:
Car-Keeper's Shop-Out Guides

Chapter 6: Customizing
Add-Ons That Subtract Years

A long-kept car, like a long-kept marriage, needs a little livening up.

Says a veteran car-keeper, "The car ran fine and I still got a kick out of driving it, just as I had the day I took delivery. But until I had it gold-striped and a sun roof added, we—that car and I—were going to the blahs."

One study, taken years ago when people traded every few years, showed that many traded in not because of growing mileage, mechanical trouble, or even styling: They simply became bored driving the same car.

The vice-president of a major mail order auto parts and accessories house estimates that "fully 25 percent of the thousands of accessories we list in our usual nearly 200-page catalog . . . are anti-blah items." He means customizing accessories—from "rear styling" conversion kits (. . . that space between your car's taillights doesn't have to be dull and uninteresting") to Porsche-style wheelcovers designed to fit very un-Porsche Volkswagen Beetles.

Detroit has for decades almost annually restyled its products because many drivers, with what researchers once called a "two-to three-year bore span" (meaning potential buyers, grown tired of their car's style, could easily be tempted to buy a new model) were vulnerable to opening their checkbooks and trading in their old for new.

Such every-few-year trading has waned to the point of eclipse, admittedly, what with the high cost of buying new, ionospheric interest rates, and demands for down payments (and superlative credit ratings), which have dramatically changed American car-buying habits.

Nonetheless, a 1981 survey still finds that 9 percent of all potential car buyers will still buy virtually anything new simply because it is new. And another 22 percent can be tempted if they spot a new model that, one way or another, is "the car of their dreams."

Such a random sampling of automotive intelligence serves as a warning to potential car-keepers: keeping a car operating miles and years longer may be easier than keeping yourself contented behind its wheel.

Among the hidden psychological barriers—and there are several—to long-term car-keeping are the automotive blahs. In time, unless you contrive to prevent it, you will almost certainly fall victim to automotive boredom: you will simply grow tired of driving the same car, day in, day out, and mile after mile. The reaction is perfectly normal. But normal or not, it can dampen, and for some cut short, the best made plans and intentions to keep a car longer.

Fortunately, veteran car-keepers—including the author—have found a cure for the blahs: customize your car and, through the years, keep adding pleasure items that

Customizing mirrors owner's life-style. Lawyer-rancher seems ready for instant shoot-out. Guns are replicas.

make the kept car unique in itself and forever rewarding to you, its owner and driver.

Customizing, for most who keep their cars, does *not* mean converting it to a hot rod or a low-rider, hanging automotive ornaments or bric-a-brac from the radiator, or reupholstering it in sheepskin. Of course, if that is your thing, and if it sustains your car-keeping interest, there's no doubt that *that*, too, is customizing. And for teen through twenties car-keepers, it obviously is.

Customizing for most, however, is far more subtle.

It means maintaining the car's sparkling and polished good looks. A just-washed car, as every operator of a car wash facility knows, does more than subtract an accumulation of dirt and road grime. It adds to the driver's own feeling of self-esteem. It makes him feel more comfortable, more prideful behind the wheel. Very likely you've experienced the feeling yourself, as you've driven from a car wash.

It means adding items of comfort, convenience, and enjoyment that, item by item, reshape the car to your own personality, tastes, and lifestyle. It may mean installing a tape deck and stereo system, a CB radio, air conditioning (if you didn't have it before), or, for computer buffs, the automotive ultimate: an in-car computer that monitors every automotive function, calculates trip mileage, records the temperature outside, reads out how much fuel you have in

the tank, tells when you need a tune-up, and acts as a speed controller. Such customizing additions are all but warranted to chase away the automotive blahs.

It means the careful, calculated restyling of your car's exterior to help erase years from its age, give it better-than-new good looks, and hand you, in time, a one-of-its-kind, personally customized driving machine. Often the calculated add-on of only a relatively few items—wheelcovers, a vinyl top, a luggage rack, professional body striping, and whitewall tires (replacing its former blacks) will do the trick. And for only a very modest investment.

Come the day that you can park in the most car-packed lot in town, yet upon your return instantly find your car from among the many, you will have achieved the ultimate blahs chaser: a customized car. That day you will have joined an ever-growing legion of contented car owners: enthusiastic car-keepers.

Sure, you may say, there's no trick in keeping it clean or having a sound shop install a stereo or a tape deck. But restyling? Come now, you've got to be joking. I'm not about to attempt to redo what the whole world knows that Detroit, Tokyo, Stuttgart, Milan, Stockholm, and Crewe do best.

No one suggests that you attempt *that* kind of restyling, nor that restyling even be considered for some makes and models.

Obviously, no owner would contemplate tampering with certain cars, whether to add or subtract, because they are either ageless or, as is and unfiddled with, nameplated with prestige. These are the vaunted "leave be" makes—Mercedes-Benz, Rolls-Royce, and the likes of the Ferrari.

Other untouchables include any of the true classic cars and even some of the neoclassics, whose very classicism depends on their being kept precisely as they came from the factory, even though they may hark back through two decades or more of model years.

The maiden year 1955 Ford Thunderbird is one of the neoclassic untouchables, as is the 1953 Chevy Corvette, first of the

Corvettes. The vintage year (1969) Pontiac Trans Am could possibly be included, and almost certainly the 1976 Cadillac Eldorado convertible—last of its line of luxury soft tops.

There are others. But by far the majority of all kept cars, including most of the imports, are ready-made for a calculated remake by their owners and drivers.

The doing is often surprisingly simple, the cost no great strain, the challenge stimulating, the shopping out of the work routine, and the results, when everything is done properly, immensely gratifying.

All of the doing can be left to add-on experts—to vinyl top installers, professional stripers, and mechanics or even filling station types adept at bolting on luggage racks or changing wheels and wheelcovers.

Still, your *own* visual judgment, backed by photo experimentation, which we'll explain a bit later, is often vital to getting the customizing done as you, the owner, want it done.

Consider just one example: the installation of a vinyl roof covering, a landau top. The doing is quick, easy, and within easy pocketbook range. *But*, because the top man charges more for a full top than for a halftop, or for something less or in between, he invariably simply suggests "a top." Almost as invariably, he means a full top—a vinyl retopping that stretches across the entire roof from the windshield to the rear window.

A full top pads his bill and pads your roof (should you elect to use a pad beneath the vinyl), but may *not* pad your driving self-esteem or your liking of the job, much less the car, once the job is installed. The reason is elementary. A full top often so restyles an older car that, instead of looking sporty, it looks older than before. Or worse, it looks like a car that has obviously been tampered with—and botched.

Good restyling enhances the original lines of a car. To the casual observer a good restyling seems factory-born to the car.

Properly restyled, your car should draw as typical a comment as did mine recently.

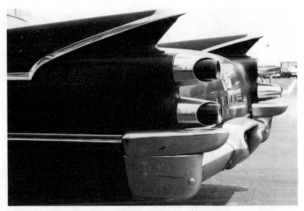

Factory-fresh long-kept car wears its chrome fins as mark of its design pedigree.

1953 Chevrolet Corvette, first of the Corvettes. (Photo courtesy of Chevrolet Motor Div., General Motors Corp.)

1955 Ford Thunderbird. (Photo courtesy of Ford Motor Company.)

"I once nearly bought a model like that one of yours," a stranger confided, ". . . and with a vinyl top just like yours." Of course he hadn't. Nor could he have! Vinyl tops were not available on my model when new. But I had succeeded, as can any car-keeper, in ordering so complementary a restyling that most people assume that it came with the car. Where that vinyl roof came from was a neighborhood top shop. The installation took less than two hours. The total cost: under $100.

To work this kind of customizing magic you needn't be a stylist, an artist, or know anything whatever about automotive design. All you need is an eye—your own

Becoming a ''car stylist'' and deciding which vinyl top will look best is as easy as ABC—A, full top; B, half-top; C, quarter top, when you snap a photo of your car, then use transparent sheet, over photo, to pen or pencil in the length of top you want. And which, using your own good judgment, will look best. Draw in all three before you tell the top man exactly the top length and style you want.

good judgment—for what looks right. And, to help you make that judgment and to avoid mistakes, you need a photo of your car. The photo, with a little penning or penciling, lets you experiment visually *before* ordering the work done. With a car photo in hand, you get a no-mistake, no-cost preview of how the job will look when finished.

The doing is easy—easy as for most such simple restyling add-ons—and especially easy when adding a vinyl top. So let's vinyl-customize your kept car's roof.

First, snap a photo—black and white or color, it doesn't matter all that much—of your car. Be sure, of course, that the photo angle shows the entire car, a side view rather than a front view. In this case, be sure to include the roof line.

Whatever the size of the print you get back from the photo shop, overlay it with some see-through material—a piece of clear plastic or tracing paper.

Now, on the overlay sheet, pen or pencil in the portion of the roof you'd like vinyl-covered. Does it look the way you had hoped it would look? If not, erase your first attempt at restyling and try again. This time, instead of a full top, pencil in only a halftop, starting about halfway back from the windshield and running to the back of the roof, just about the rear window.

Looks better? Probably it does. On some cars as little as a quarter roofing—starting three-quarters of the way back from the windshield and again going to the rear window—looks best of all, giving a car its sportiest, going-places look.

Once you've decided from your photo preplanning what will look and work best, it's a good idea to do a layout on the car's roof.

Scissors, some wrapping paper (or even newspaper), and a roll of masking tape comprise your total stylist kit. Cut the paper to the approximate size of the roof area you've decided to have vinyl-covered and, using the masking tape, tape your template in place.

Now, stand back and take a hard look. Does it look as your photo preplanning told

A top man installs your vinyl roof, but you tell him—after photo and template experimentation—whether you want a full roof topping or something less.

you it would look? Chances are it looks even better. A three-dimensional roof lay-up like that often does.

On the other hand, with the template taped to your rooftop, you may decide the look is not quite right. A few inches more or less, your eye tells you, would look even better.

Trust your own judgment. In visual restyling—and that is what you are doing—a few inches either way can make a very considerable visual difference. The total overall visual effect is what you're after. You do whatever seems to help that effect.

If you've decided a few inches less would look better, snip an inch or two from the template. Or, with masking tape, add a few inches.

Step back once again and have another look. "Precisely right," you tell yourself. And that is what you will tell the installer. But rather than merely tell him, and risk his either making a mistake or deciding he knows better than you do (he usually does not), *mark* the place on the car's roof, with a piece of masking tape, where you want the vinyl roofing to begin.

Then, when you drive into the top shop, ask the installer to estimate the cost for a vinyl roof for the area you've marked. And you'll get the job done—and the restyling installed—the way your own good visual judgment, photo and template aided, told you it would look best.

Most subtle customizing jobs are as easy as that.

Almost always, the "try it first" approach is the way to go.

Suppose your next attempt at restyling is striping. You want vinyl striping applied along the car's body. While it is possible to use very thin—say ⅛-inch wide—masking tape to see how the stripes will look once in place, a better idea is to observe striping on other cars. When you see a striping job you particularly admire, haul out your camera and snap some quick pictures. When you take the car in for striping you need only hand the striper you photos and tell him, "I want striping that looks like this."

Or, take the case of wheelcovers, which dress up a car to an often gratifying degree. Whether you shop an auto junkyard or the swankiest auto sport shop in town, borrow a cover and place it beside one wheel of the car. That way you'll see how it—and three more covers just like it—will look when installed.

The right wheelcovers can do wonders in de-aging and upgrading the appearance of any car. The wrong covers may make you shudder. Sometimes, to pick precisely the right covers for your wheels, you may need visually to test a dozen different styles and designs. Inevitably, one will work for your car.

Pretesting is worth the time it takes. The penalty for not pretesting is apt to be disappointment. Too often the results fall short—sometimes far short—of the customized appearance you had in mind. So let's look at what might be called "the car-keeper's styling bag of tricks." By any reckoning, it is a modest bag—in cost and numbers. Involved are no real tricks, simply hardheaded judgment of what, for you, will banish the car-keeping blahs.

Listed are a few basic, right-priced, easily added styling items that can help personalize the kept car. Added gradually, they customize, sometimes also protecting paint and chrome, add exterior luggage space, beautify, and, ideally, convert a Detroit, Tokyo, or Paris product to a one-of-its-kind personal driving machine.

Trim/Rub Molding

These are the so-called *rub strips*, vinyl or rubber, variable-width (available from about ⁷⁄₁₆ inch to 1⅜ inches wide), protective but also customizing strips, one usually run along each side of the vehicle and fitted into a screw-on aluminum channel. The rub-strips protect body paint from suddenly opened adjacent car doors. Although available in a wide range of colors, including black, what looks best is usually a color that comes closest to matching your car's paint. They are available from installers: auto paint and striping shops.

Luggage Rack (Rear Deck or Rooftop Mount)

This bolts to the rear deck (trunk lid) or to the roof, adding strap-on luggage space if you need it. But a rack's more persuasive use in customizing is decorative rather than utilitarian.

Racks vary widely in quality, design, strength, and cost. Pick the right luggage rack, meaning one that is (1) big enough to appear, at casual glance, as though it were an OEM item (one that came originally with the car); (2) sturdy enough to carry luggage if need be; (3) quality-chromed, just as are most of a car's original factory-chromed parts. Even some relatively expensive add-on luggage racks ($80–$150 for rear deck models, more for the roof mount) are thinly chromed. After a few years they may begin to rust. Quality racks

Roof rack adds a sporty flair to any car, particularly to one suffering from unsportiness.

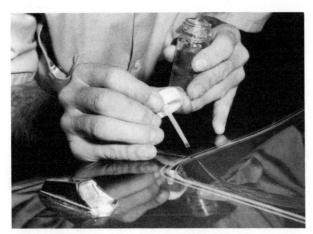

After vinyl striping is applied, striping is given a seal coat, preserving stripe life for years.

In customizing, wheelcovers help dress up an older car. You'll find wheelcovers by the million at auto dismantling places.

are available at auto specialty stores, notably sports car/import shops. Racks are installed by top and body shops, occasionally by auto accessory stores.

Striping

Microthin, colored plastic or Mylar striping ribbon, the modern-day version of the hand striper's art, can do more to update and customize a car than virtually any other single add-on item. But only a pro striper can do the job correctly (he also carries a wide choice of colors, widths, designs). Once applied, stripes are overpainted with clear lacquer or a polyurethane-type plastic finish. Done correctly, stripes stay put for years. Done wrong, they can peel and chip.

Pro stripers shun the adhesive-backed, self-sticking stripes like the plague, and so should you. If a striping shop isn't listed in your phone book, ask a local luxury car dealer (such as Cadillac, Lincoln, etc.) for the name of his striper. Should his recommendation turn out to be an old-school hand striper, fine. But painted-on stripes may lack the durability of the vinyl.

Wheelcovers and Wheels

Available is a seemingly endless variety of decor-customizing wheels (chromed, "mag"-magnesium, others) and their even

fancier dressings, wheelcovers. Fanciest, and most expensive, are the wire wheels or covers, which are in such popular demand by wheel thieves that if you go wire, also get security locks for each wheel or cover.

If your car doesn't already wear them, you may prefer OEMs (the factory-original covers). You can sometimes find them in heavy, original factory chrome or stainless steel at auto junk-parts yards. Clean them up with chrome or metal polish. And you'll have bought a bargain: the same customizing visual effect as buying new but at far less cost. No one but you will know the difference. These are installed wherever tires and wheels are installed, including your neighborhood service station.

Vinyl Top, Sun Roof, Louvered Rear Window Sunshield, Whitewall Tires, "Bras"

These are all items with maximum customizing effect and impact for kept cars. And that includes the "bra," the front-end rock/debris/bug protective cover that helps dress up (though from its name you'd never guess it) some of the sportier cars, including the imports.

All of these customizing accessories are available in various styles, sometimes in body-matching colors, with installation (except for the install-it-yourself "bra") best left to specialists. That applies in particular to sun roofs, either the expensive in-roof type or the more modest-priced pop-ups. Sun roof installation is almost always tedious. A so-so job hands you a "leaker": a car with a leaky roof. Top shops can install rear window sunshields as well as vinyl tops. Whitewalls, as all tires, should be spin-balanced, *not* hand-balanced, by a competent tire shop.

And there you have it: a sampling of customizers that, item for item, have maximum visual impact for kept cars.

Actually, the list of customizing accessories is as long as the index in any auto supply catalog or the wall-to-wall display racks in any auto store. The canniest car-keepers ignore the temptation to overpersonalize and overgadgetize. Besides, many of the "hot items" in the catalogs and parts houses are "price goods": cheaply crafted, short on durability, and little more than enticing gimmicks.

Subtle customizing is not gimmickry. Certainly the add-on of some of the items we've listed can substantially update a car. Nor need you spend more than your strategy schedule budgeting allows in doing so.

Advises an old hand at customizing, "It is far better, month by month, even year by year, to have installed a single quality customizing item—say a vinyl top or a sun roof—than to add on a clutter of cheapies. The quality lasts. The cheapies seldom do."

A rush to customize often leads one to clutterize, negating the whole concept of a personalized driving machine that, to casual observers, doesn't seem added to at all.

This kept car wears a "bra"—front-end protector against rock and road debris damage to finish.

The louvered look—a customizer for any kept car.

The doing requires time, thought, patience, and planning. But when it's done, you'll be proud of yourself (you've become a stylist, using easily available items) and proud of your car (it's more fun to drive now).

Thus, self-sustained, this is the kind of car-keeping excitement that's all but guaranteed to chase the blahs.

Chapter 7: Engine
Restoring Its Power

In the strategy of keeping a car longer, one reminder is worth fixing to the dashboard: "Don't panic!" When it concerns the engine, too many normally coolheaded car-keepers do.

In a way, that's odd. Granted, the engine is the heart of your car, yet only rarely does any kind of internal engine trouble stop a car dead or force one of those immediate and painful out-of-pocket decisions: rebuild the engine or dump the car. Other problems that *do* stop a car dead in its treads seemingly cause far less concern. And they almost never flash, in the mind of the car owner, an instant panic choice between repair and disposal.

Break a *driveline* (on rear-wheel-powered cars, the shaft that powers the wheels), and you're dead on the highway.

Abuse the *manual transmission* to the point of gear stripping, and likely you'll find yourself stopped. Lose the gears in the *automatic transmission*, and, in many instances, the car won't move or it will hardly move at all.

Develop any of numerous other troubles—from *ignition switch* failure (no longer is there an electrical connection between the battery and the engine's *starter motor*) to a failed *fuel pump*—and your car's a no-go.

By contrast, with very few exceptions, engine trouble and engine wear-out come on gradually, permitting months, even years, of calculated car-keeping stretch-out *before* you have to invest in, or seriously concern yourself with, certainly the largest investment in automotives: an engine overhaul, rebuild, or replacement. (See interview, "An Expert Explains Engine Rebuilding," on page 64).

Yet millions of drivers have been panicked by a gasoline station attendant's doleful conclusion, "Lady, your engine's using oil."

Of course it is. All engines do. Yours, if the attendant is correct, is simply using more oil than it should. A quart, perhaps, every 300–400 miles instead of, when new, every 750–1,000 miles. And, yes, oil use, along with other telltale signs—a gradual diminishing of power, blue-colored exhaust smoke, and poor gasoline mileage, to mention but three—all suggest, and sometimes signal, the onset of engine trouble.

Not only could these signs be false (they sometimes are) and the pump jockey's diagnosis fallacious (were he an engine expert, he'd be manning a wrench, at three times his present pay, rather than a gas pump), but few of these signs of portending trouble signal engine problems with any real immediacy.

If you can accept adding oil a bit more frequently, spending a little more for gasoline and driving with less get-up-and-go than when the car was new, you can—as do the canniest of those who keep their cars miles and years longer—drive thousands of miles more before facing a major engine decision.

Why, then, are so many potential car-keepers—and those who planned to be—panicked into getting rid of their car merely because it is using more oil, more gasoline, and is less powerful than 40,000 miles ago?

Bluntly, it is because, knowing virtually nothing about their engine's innards, they assume that a noticeable increase in oil use, for one, means the engine is due for a quick death and that, not too far down the road, it will simply stop. Or, worse, it will grind itself to pieces en route.

Nonsense. Most often it merely means that, like anything mechanical (or even human), it is showing signs of natural and inevitable age. In human terms, having run through youth and puberty between 0 and 20,000 miles, and progressed into adulthood and middle age between 30,000 and 50,000 miles, it is verging on senior citizenship. But it is still miles—perhaps 30,000–70,000 miles—from shuffling old age.

Nonetheless, persistent signs of engine aging and performance deterioration, as a persistent human pain, should suggest that you see a specialist—an engine specialist. For an often quick, accurate, and honest engine diagnosis, here are three possible specialist choices:

Engine Specialist. Opt for a mechanic, and far better if he is a mechanic you know and trust, who makes engines his workaday specialty. He may charge nothing—a "friendly" mechanic usually will not—for the five to 15 minutes it takes to make the few simple tests that tell a great deal about your engine's innards.

One of the most telling tests—using a *compression gauge* to check the compression in each of the engine's cylinders—is so quick, simple, and easily understood, even by those who know or care little about engines, that any car owner can understand the test's findings. You can also stand over the mechanic while he makes the test, virtually reading the gauge right along with him. (See "Ring and Valve Job: Need It or Not?" page 69.)

Do your kept car's rings and valves really need repair? While you watch, mechanic makes engine compression test to find out. (Photo courtesy of Fram Corporation.)

Diagnostic Center. Take your car to one of the shops that makes it its business to diagnose (*not* repair) automotive, and especially engine, problems or the lack of them. Since diagnosis is a true diagnostic center's only source of revenue, there is, of course, a charge for testing your engine. These centers can also, if you wish, test other parts of the car.

Again, engine diagnosis is usually made while you wait. And, since the diagnosis-only auto centers do no repairs, and thus don't stand to profit from unnecessary work-finding, their findings are apt to be scrupulously honest. They are often among the first to reassure the panicked, "Nothing is really wrong that won't wait a lot of miles more."

Engine Tune-Up Shop. These, generally franchised or chain operations sprung up now almost everywhere (Tuneup Masters and others), are among the most-for-your-money engine diagnostic places. And for a number of reasons.

First, like diagnostic centers, they use the latest electronic engine analyzers.

Second, they do no engine work, just

engine tune-up. And they risk losing a customer with a sick-engined car because, should that be their diagnosis, most of the tune-up shops will not guarantee the tune-up for the usual six months as many now do. One of their customer pleasers is that six-month guarantee, which permits you, anytime during that period, to bring the car back for further fiddling without further charge. If your engine is diagnosed sick, the shop can obviously not guarantee that its tune-up will remain effective over the normal guarantee period. Whatever the verdict, it is the product of advanced electronic analysis. And it is made while you wait.

Third, good diagnosis or bad, your engine gets a tune-up. So you get both a diagnosis and an engine tune for your money. And the cost—a fixed price depending on the number of cylinders—is modest.

Wherever you go, however, the problem for many car-keepers is understanding, much less making sense of, what the diagnostic specialist says is wrong (if anything) with your engine. Understanding the mechanic's or diagnostician's vocabulary is a first step toward understanding your choices in restoring your engine's power.

Here, then, is a minicourse in easily understood fundamentals: how and why an engine works and why, as the miles and years go by, it may no longer work as well. Gasoline and diesel engines work the same way, up to a point. When that point is reached, we'll briefly explain the diesel difference.

Your engine is a *reciprocating* engine, as contrasted to other types of engines you've heard about, such as rotary or turbine engines. *Reciprocating* means that within the engine something goes up and down to power something that goes around and around.

The *pistons* are the things that go up and down. Each piston works within a *cylinder*. The pistons' up and down travel within the cylinders is used to drive something around and around, that something being the *crankshaft*, which turns your car's wheels through gearing.

Your engine is also an *internal combustion* engine, which means that all of the combustion (the explosion of the *carburetor*-supplied gasoline and air fuel mix, when ignited by the *spark plugs*) takes place internally, within the engine.

Where the combustion takes place is usually a tiny space at the top of each cylinder, above the top of each piston. This space is called the *combustion chamber*. Actually, in many engines, it is not a special chamber, just a space at the top of the cylinders.

In precise *firing order*, the pistons move up and down within their cylinders. What powers each piston's up and down travel within its cylinder is the tremendous force of the explosion of fuel and air in the cylinder's combustion chamber. It is a ham-

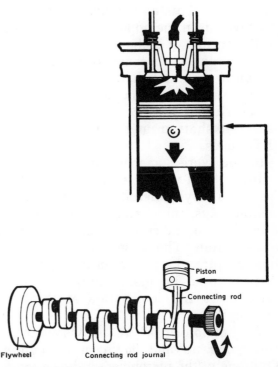

Crankshaft is the engine maestro. It is the only part in the engine that knows all the engine players—and if they are playing in tune. For the crankshaft is the only part connected to or driving every other engine part, such as the pistons. Shown is how a piston is connected to the crankshaft and how the piston, slammed downward by the force of the detonation in the combustion chamber above it, helps to power the crankshaft and thus the car's wheels. (Drawing courtesy of Caterpillar Tractor Co.)

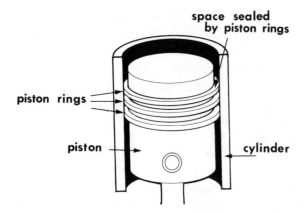

If the mechanic is correct in saying that your engine needs a "ring job," he means that the piston rings no longer seal the space between the piston and the cylinder wall. If true, he'll have to replace the piston rings with new ones, which do seal the space. (Drawing courtesy of Caterpillar Tractor Co.)

merlike detonation that, once the piston has reached close to the top of its cylinder, forces the piston suddenly to travel downward, in the opposite direction. Fixed to the bottom of each piston is a *connecting rod*, so named because it connects each piston to the crankshaft.

Thus, as each piston moves up and down it contributes its force and power to turn the crankshaft around and around, driving the wheels.

If you were somehow to peer into each cylinder, you would see what the mechanics are always dolefully talking about: the *piston rings*, the circular metal rings, usually three or more of them, fitted around each piston. The rings, which circle the pistons just like a ring on a finger, play a critical role in maintaining the power created by the combustion at the top of each cylinder.

Why piston rings? Well, envisage the piston going up and down in its cylinder. Obviously, the piston cannot be as large in diameter as the cylinder in which it moves, or the piston wouldn't move. It would stick. Thus the piston is considerably smaller in diameter than the cylinder in which it works. So what have you got? A space between the piston and the cylinder's wall. *That* space has kept a lot of mechanics in business and helped panic many car-

keepers. What fills—and seals—this space are the piston rings. That is their sole business and their reason for being.

If they fail to do their job, the cylinder, and your car's engine, loses *compression*—some of the power created by the explosion of fuel in the cylinder's combustion chamber. But piston ring failure causes many other problems: increasing oil use, greater fuel consumption, and lower engine power and performance. Let's see why.

The piston rings, for whatever else they do, act as buffers between two opposing forces, both of them trying to get through that space between the piston and its cylinder wall.

One force is the enormous explosion—*above the piston*—in the combustion chamber. The force and heat of the gasoline detonation reach outward and downward. Were it not for the piston rings, much of this explosive force would squeeze through the piston-to-cylinder space and be wasted. Instead of exerting its powerful force on the top of the piston, much of the power created by the gasoline detonation would escape through that piston-to-cylinder space and would be lost.

The other force trying to squeeze through the space the piston rings are attempting to seal comes from *below the piston*, from the engine's main oil reservoir, which is contained by the *oil pan*.

Oil is forever being forced upward under high pressure (by the *oil pump*) to bathe the cylinders, the pistons, and their rings with lubrication. Without lubrication the pistons and their rings would quickly grow fiery hot—and as quickly seize. More than simply stopped, the pistons and their rings might even melt and bond themselves to the cylinder walls.

Now, so long as the piston rings are operating as they should, they stand as a barrier—the *only* barrier—between the two opposing forces working within each cylinder.

From below, oil is being forced upward. Its force is great enough to break through the piston ring barrier unless the piston rings are sealing perfectly. From above, the forces of detonation are likewise trying to break through the piston ring barrier, and they can, unless the piston rings are sealing perfectly. And for the first many thousands of miles, most piston rings—incredibly—do.

Eventually, however, they begin to wear—through old age or far sooner through abrasive oil contamination, unless you frequently have the oil and its oil filter changed.

As piston rings gradually wear, they gradually fail to seal, as well as before, the space they were designed to seal. What happens is pretty self-evident. Oil from below slips by the rings and into the combustion chamber, where it burns. As the rings wear more and more, more and more oil slips past them and is burnt. And your engine begins needing more and more oil, more and more frequently.

"You're burning oil," the mechanic tells you. And he is probably correct. Actually, if you have observed *blue smoke* coming out of your exhaust pipe, and if you know what it signals, you already know the engine is burning oil. Blue smoke is from oil burning.

But just as oil from below slips past wearing or broken piston rings, so do some of the gases from the combustion chamber above. Those gases represent power. Their loss through the rings means power loss. And that means fuel waste. You begin to notice that you fill up more often—that you're getting fewer miles to the gallon.

You also are losing *compression* in the cylinder, or the several, whose piston rings are failing.

Since the piston rings no longer seal as well as before, the piston has lost some of its ability to *compress* and contain air within the cylinder, and particularly within the cylinder's combustion chamber.

"Madam, you have *blowby*," diagnoses the mechanic, meaning neither an obscenity nor anything personal. Quite literally, his diagnosis is correct, some of the combustion chamber's compressed gases—the stuff of its power—are "blowing by" the piston rings and are being lost.

Loss of compression is another way of saying that a cylinder has lost its ability to contribute, toward powering the car, the full power it was meant to contribute.

If the oil seepage from below, past the piston rings, is considerable, unburnt oil or its burnt residue, carbon, may actually impinge on the spark plug's *electrodes*. These are the electrical terminals between which the battery's electricity flows each time the spark plug *fires*.

If enough oil or carbon collects on the spark plug's electrodes, the spark plug will no longer fire. It will fail to ignite the fuel and air mix in its combustion chamber.

"Your engine is *missing*," the mechanic diagnoses. He doesn't mean, of course, that it has disappeared or been stolen. He means that possibly at least one cylinder is no longer functioning.

There are other, far simpler, reasons why a spark plug may not fire, and thus, why a cylinder may be missing. For one, there may be an electrical short in the wire that powers the spark plug. The wire comprises part of the *electrical harness* that carries electricity to each spark plug. Or, the spark plug itself may be old and dirty, or even cracked, and need to be replaced.

Whatever the reason, if your engine is missing, you already are aware of the problem. A "missing" cylinder—unbalancing the smooth operation of the engine—causes the

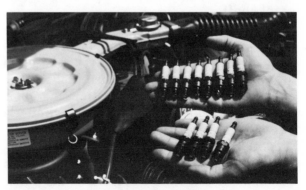

If engine "misses" (a cylinder isn't being fired by its spark plug), the failure represents 25 percent of the four-cylinder engine's power, but only 12½ percent if the same thing happens in an eight-cylinder engine. Spark plugs in four-cylinder engine work far harder than plugs in the larger engine. (Photo courtesy of Fram Corporation.)

car to shake, especially when the engine is idling, and also, of course, to have less power. The engine, after all, is operating with fewer cylinders than it was designed to operate with.

In an eight-cylinder engine the loss of a single cylinder, which represents only 12½ percent of the engine's total power, may sometimes be scarcely noticeable, particularly at cruising speeds. But in a four-cylinder engine loss of a cylinder represents a power loss of 25 percent—one-fourth of its original power. And though the car will probably go, it hardly goes at all.

Finally, there are the *valves*, which are precisely what their name implies: moving parts that intermittently open and close.

Most cylinders have two valves, mounted in the *head* of the engine, which is bolted to the engine's *block*, just above the top of the cylinders.

The valves close to seal the combustion chamber tightly shut during the moment of fuel detonation and open to permit escape from the combustion chamber of the spent fumes and gases after the detonation. All of these spent by-products of combustion, including heat, are collected in a common *exhaust manifold* and vented from the engine through the *exhaust pipe* and its anti-pollution devices.

As are all other major internal engine parts, the valves, though remotely, are controlled—opened and closed—by the crankshaft.

The crankshaft *knows* at every microsecond what no other single part of the engine can know: where every piston is along its cylinder travel, when fuel and air are metered into the combustion chamber, and when to open and close each cylinder's valves.

As a kind of engine maestro, the crankshaft conducts all of the engine's players through their intricate score and has a mechanical sixth sense for those who, through fault or failure, attempt to improvise.

Long before the automobile engines had computers, the crankshaft was the engine's mechanical computer. And not because it was mechanically smarter than any other

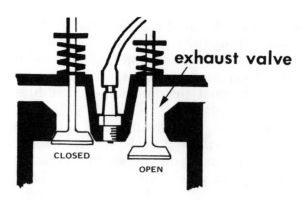

Do you need a valve job? Maybe. Valves, in engine's head, above cylinders, must perfectly open and close, helped to perfect seating on their valve seats by springlike valve guides. Here, moments after detonation in cylinder's combustion chamber, the exhaust valve of each cylinder's pair of valves has opened to permit escape of combustion chamber spent gases. (Drawing courtesy of Caterpillar Tractor Co.)

part but simply because every moving part in the engine is either physically connected to the crankshaft—each piston, through its connecting rod, for example—or, through gearing, chains, or other means, directly controlled by the crankshaft.

What controls the opening and closing of the valves is the *camshaft*. This, too, is driven by the crankshaft.

If anything, the valves play an even more critical role in sealing the combustion chamber against escape of its enormous—and power-providing—forces than do the piston rings.

The valves must, *before* every combustion, perfectly seal themselves on their *valve seats*, which are also in the engine's *head*, just above the combustion chambers. Perfectly mated, the valve and its seat combine to seal shut the combustion chamber.

After each detonation the valves must just as precisely and instantly open to vent into the engine's exhaust the hot by-products of the combustion.

To seal perfectly, the valve's *face* must be perfectly flat. Just as perfectly flat must be its *seat*. The mating of the two must be like a 60-year marriage—only far better. Helping each valve to remain perfectly perpendicular to its seat, thus to ensure the perfect mating of the two, is a *valve guide*. It guides and helps the valve to its seat.

If the sealing and seating are not perfect, some combustion chamber gases—the pent-up power of the cylinder—escape through the valve opening. En route to escape, the hot gases may, little by little, burn and distort the valve's face, its seat, and even its guide. In time, because the surface flatness of both valve partners becomes more and more impaired, their ability to seal becomes more and more imperfect. And the engine's power loss becomes greater and greater.

"We'll have to grind the valves," the mechanic tells you. Or he may call it *a valve job.* Whatever his choice of words, he means he will have to remove the valves and have their faces and seats machine-ground once again to perfect flatness.

A diesel engine, too, has valves, pistons, piston rings, cylinders. In fact, a diesel and a gasoline engine operate in the same way, but with some sizable, mostly combustion chamber, differences.

At casual glance the two engines may, to the uninitiated, look alike. Their differences are more internal than external.

Designed to produce often twice the compression—thus twice the internal pressure—as a gasoline engine, the diesel's pistons compress air, and nothing more, into the cylinder's combustion chambers. Compression alone, as every basic physics course teaches, produces heat. In the case of the diesel, it is fiery heat.

At the instant that the compressed air, in any of a diesel's combustion chambers, reaches a temperature hot enough to ignite almost anything within fiery reach, diesel fuel is *injected* into the chamber. *Heat of compression* alone ignites the fuel.

Thus, the diesel has no need for the gasoline engine's fueling and ignition devices—carburetor, distributor, points, spark plugs, and all of the other paraphernalia that induce and trigger combustion within a gas engine's cylinders.

Plain and simply, the diesel combusts spontaneously the moment that its cylinders' compressed, fiery air is injected with fuel.

The diesel's remarkable fuel economy stems directly from its ability to compress air—still one of the world's few no-cost commodities—to the point of ignition, something no gasoline engine can do. The diesel, moreover, actually derives some of its piston power from the air it compresses. Thus, the diesel "burns" a huge quantity of air and a relatively small quantity of fuel. By nature, the diesel is among the most fuel-economical of engines.

And so, in understandable terms, you have—as must any car-keeper—glimpsed the inner workings of your car's engine. You've also learned some of the vocabulary—and some of the lingo—of the mechanic and garageman.

The engine work the mechanic says you need may not be needed at all. But now, with most of the mystique stripped from the auto engine, you will no longer sign his work order without some hard questioning. Nor, in most cases, will you do so without demanding that he perform, as you watch, that simplest but most revealing of inner-engine health tests. (See, "Ring and Valve Job: Need It or Not?" page 69.)

Engine trouble? It may lie miles down the road. Should it come, however, you are forearmed.

INTERVIEW: AN EXPERT EXPLAINS ENGINE REBUILDING

M. E. "Monty" Thill is recognized as a consummate engine expert. As the longtime general manager of one of the largest engine rebuilders — Motor Machine & Supply, Inc. — he has overseen the rebuilding of thousands of automobile engines. Here, in excerpted interview, he shares his insight with car-keepers.

Thill: Power loss, a common driver complaint, is sending a lot of car owners to engine mechanics and rebuilders when the problem may not be in the engine at all. It may be in the fuel the engine is burning.

Q: The gasoline available at the pumps today is different from the gas of just a few years back?

Thill: Far different. And right there's one reason for noticeable power loss. Today, the power rating of most 'regular' gasoline is down around 87 octane. It used to be closer to 100 — and sometimes higher. And the no-lead isn't nowadays much higher in octane than the 'regular.'

Q: Then the power loss car-keepers may be experiencing — less power from their kept cars than those same cars had a few years back — may not mean a 'sick' engine but, maybe 'sick' fuel?

Thill: Absolutely. And when you also take the lead out, something else happens. Now, lead in gasoline does two things, primarily. It acts as an upper engine lubricant. And it slows down the burning rate of the fuel mix so that you get a more complete fuel burn. And that, in itself, extracts more power from the fuel.

Q: So, lower octane rating plus no-lead means less power?

Thill: Considerably less, and the more noticeable in eight-cylinder cars, in cars that normally had a lot of power. But, in fact, this is true in any engine — whatever the number of cylinders. Making the power loss even worse — and more noticeable — are the leaner fuel mixes almost all engines are now burning.

Q: Leaner? That is, less gasoline, but more air is nowadays introduced, through the carburetor, into a gasoline engine's firing chambers — into its cylinders?

Thill: Right. In order to meet federal fuel economy requirements, the manufacturers specify a leaner fuel mix: a higher ratio of air to gasoline.

Q: More air, less fuel — to achieve fuel economy?

Thill: Yes. But there's a penalty: less performance. When the fuel an engine burns is 'leaned' — carburetor-mixed to contain as little fuel as possible — you simply can't get from an engine the horsepower it's designed to produce.

An engine doesn't run on air. Nor, in a gasoline engine, does it really extract any power from air. So the leaner — the higher the air content to the gasoline content of the fuel mix — the less power an engine can develop.

Certainly, your mileage per gallon is better. But your engine's performance is worse.

Q: Inevitably, of course, engines do need work — rebuilding or even replacement?

Thill: In time, yes, but that time can be stretched miles and years farther down the road if the engine, right along, and from the very start, is kept clean.

Q: Oil changed at the mileage or time intervals prescribed in the owner's manual?

Thill: *Far* sooner, generally, than that. We get engines in here every day that have been 'oil changed by the book,' meaning as specified in an owner's manual. Or changed according to oil company claims, for some of their newer oils, that you can run it twice as long as ever before without changing it. Well, their oil may hold up, but the engines don't.

Q: Why not?

Thill: One word explains why not: dirt. An engine continuously contaminates itself. Every detonation in the cylinders creates soot and other by-products of combustion. And moving metal parts forever slough off tiny metal particles. The fact that they are 'suspended' in an oil doesn't mean they aren't damaging an engine and shortening its life, hastening the day when you've got to spend a very considerable amount of money repairing the damage.

Q: So, while the newer oils, or even some of the older ones, may look great under a laboratory microscope, the oil is 'holding up,' oil carries engine-wearing particles created by the engine itself . . . and, in time, the engine itself may not 'hold up'?

Thill: Exactly. That's why you can't say, 'Change the oil and put in a new oil filter every 3,000 miles' or 'every 6,000 miles' or whatever. To get the full 90,000–100,000 miles of minimum maintenance service out of the average automobile engine, you've got to change the oil, and probably the oil filter, *whenever the oil needs it.*

Q: When the oil is dirty?

Thill: Right. And you don't have to know a thing about engines to know when the oil is dirty. *If it isn't clean, it's dirty.* Every time you add oil or have someone add it, look at a little of the oil on the oil measuring dipstick. If it looks dirty, change it, even if you last changed just 500 miles ago. And if you drive, perhaps just over a weekend, in a dusty, windy area, take a look at that dipstick oil sample again when you get home. Chances are the oil will look grimy, because, having picked up a lot of dust and sand, which are among the most abrasive of engine contaminants, it *is* grimy. It's loaded, despite everything the filter can do, with sand and dirt. *Change oil* — even if you changed oil only yesterday.

Q: That can get pretty expensive, can't it?

Thill: Not nearly as expensive as major engine work.

Q: That brings up the potentially 'big buck' decision a car-keeper may one day have to make: major engine repair. What, roughly, is involved in 'rebuilding' an engine, say, as compared to 'overhauling' it?

Thill: When you talk about major engine work you run, I admit, into a problem: vocabulary. What one mechanic calls a 'rebuild' may really be an 'overhaul.' And what we call a 'remanufacturing job' may differ from them both.

Q: Well, if mechanics and engine repair industry people haven't clearly defined what they do, and what they deliver for the money, how would you expect the average car-keeper to know what he or she is getting and paying for?

Thill: Two ways.

First, no matter how little you know or care about engines, you obviously care if the work is really needed. And, if so, how much it's going to cost. Insofar as whether the work is needed, for the most routine of all engine work, the so-called 'ring and valve job,' there's a simple test that the mechanic can make with you standing over him — a test anybody can understand. Simple as the test is, it tells whether the work is needed.

Second, whatever the engine repair, don't settle for a label, whether the mechanic calls it an 'overhaul' or a 'rebuild' or something else. Get in writing a specific list of things he is going to do.

Q: Most car-keepers, who aren't engine buffs or do-it-yourselfers, would have trouble with that one. A mechanic could write down virtually anything, and the car owner, not being a mechanic or knowing engine parts or terms, couldn't dispute it.

Thill: I think most car owners could, with just a little inkling — if they don't already have it — of what an engine, *their* engine, is all about.

Q: The ABCs of any car owner's engine, using terms most owners are already familiar with?

Thill: Precisely. Terms the mechanic uses when he explains the work an engine needs. Knowing them — and knowing when the mechanic is using them properly — could mean the difference between okaying a job costing a few hundred dollars and one costing upwards of $1,000 or more.

Q: Essentially, then, we are merely defining some words with which most car-keepers are already familiar?

Thill: Exactly. And, hopefully, in a way that will pretty much simplify any car owner's engine.

Functionally, you can think of an automotive engine as having two sections, one bolted atop the other.

The *bottom* section, called the *block,* is by far the largest, heaviest, and most expensive part of an engine to repair. Basically, it is the *power-producing* section.

In it, you have the *cylinders,* in which the *pistons* move up and down, the space between each piston and the wall of its cylinder being sealed by *piston rings.*

Now, as they move up and down within their cylinders, the pistons transmit their power through *connecting rods,* which turn the *crankshaft.* The crankshaft, through gearing and the transmission, which are not part of the engine, turns the wheels.

Q: Terms every car-keeper is certainly familiar with?

Thill: Sometimes, painfully — in the pocketbook — so.

The *upper* bolt-on part of an engine, called the *head,* is the *power-controlling* section.

It's far smaller, contains smaller parts, and is easier and cheaper to repair than the bottom engine section and its heavier, often more expensive parts.

For one thing, when a mechanic needs to repair something in the engine's bottom section, he's got to take off the top section, the head — which takes time, running up the labor bill — just to get to the bottom section and its parts.

In this upper section are, among other power-controlling parts, the *valves.*

The valves, mechanically opened and closed by *cams,* which in turn are controlled by the crankshaft in the lower part of the engine, continuously open and close to control the combustion in each *combustion chamber,* which is in the top of each cylinder.

As combustion-power controllers, the valves are the real criticals in the upper engine (head) power-control section.

Q: Very basically, without getting into the combustion part of it — how fuel and air in the combustion chamber are ignited by the spark plugs — you've pretty well defined the engine basics?

Thill: The internal engine's main parts and what they do and how they work together, yes.

Q: And the parts that seem to go wrong first and fastest in an engine are the *piston rings* in the lower part of the engine and the *valves* in the upper part?

Thill: That's right. And so the mechanic tells the car owner he proposes to do a 'ring and valve job.'

Q: Meaning?

Thill: That he's going to replace worn or faulty piston rings and correct any malfunction of the upper-engine valves.

Q: He can do this 'in engine' — with the engine still in the vehicle?

Thill: Yes, though, of course, he's got to take off the upper part of the engine, the head, to reach the block, the engine's lower part, where the cylinders, the pistons, and the piston rings are.

Q: But suppose involved are more than just piston rings and valves. Suppose the mechanic tells the car keeper the engine needs an 'overhaul.' What does he mean?

Thill: Well, he could still be talking about just a 'ring and valve job,' which is why you've got to get down, in writing, exactly what he does plan to do.

But, probably, when he recommends an 'overhaul,' he really means that the engine needs to be 'rebuilt' — all of its parts that are faulty or failing either replaced with new or corrected, perhaps by machining them, so that the engine once again functions correctly.

Q: Is the average mechanic capable of 'rebuilding' an engine — of quite literally tearing it apart, fixing what needs to be fixed, and putting it all back together again?

Thill: A really competent mechanic can; no doubt about that. The problem, especially for a car owner who doesn't know or care much about engines or mechanics, is finding *that* competent mechanic.

Q: That, and knowing beforehand, if at all possible, what so extensive an engine 'rebuild' will cost?

Thill: Yes. So before going ahead with a job as large as that a car owner should consider his options.

Q: There are options . . . other than simply telling the mechanic, 'Tear it down,' and all but writing him a blank check?

Thill: A number of them, yes.

He can, of course, have the mechanic do the job. And if the mechanic is competent and honest, there is no reason why the car owner will not get a good job. Whether it is the 'best' job he can buy, and for the least money, is another matter.

Or, figuring if he's going to spend considerable money anyway, he might as well get a fresh-from-the-factory engine — or a part of it, depending on what's needed — he can have the mechanic or a car dealership order him an OEM (Original Engine Manufacturer) factory engine. A brand-new factory engine, or just part of it.

In some cases, what's wrong is mainly in the bottom part of the engine. So he would need to buy only what the trade calls a *short block,* a brand-new power-producing engine section (block). If he needs, as well, the engine's top power-controlling section (the head), then he would order a *long block,* which is the *complete* engine, ready to install in the car. But brand-new factory engines — whether the whole (long block) or the half (short block) — are very expensive. Probably not many car-keepers can cost-justify the factory-new engine option.

Q: And, of course, it is possible to buy a used engine — say, a low-mileage engine that somehow survived unscathed from a car-totaling, a nearly car-destroying, accident?

Thill: As options go, for those who need a re-engining, that's probably the least desirable. Now, those who know engines can, and occasionally do, find such a prize. But documenting a used engine's mileage history — its true mileage — is always dif-

ficult. The thing is, picking up a really good survivor — an engine in excellent condition, with low mileage, despite the accident the car has been in — is the kind of thing done best by those who are very conversant with engines.

Q: And, like the legendary automotive 'cream puffs,' cars supposedly driven only by little old dowagers, any but a very knowledgeable engine buyer can be 'cream puffed': touted to an engine that has far more miles and wear than its seller is willing to admit?

Thill: Yes. I would want to know far more about a used engine, however, than merely its true mileage, assuming you can document even that. I would want to know, from its very first mile, how it was maintained — when and if oil and oil filter changes were made. A neglected engine with 5,000 documented miles of *use* could very well have 10,000, even 25,000, undocumented miles of *wear.*

Q: Still, let me give you one example of how, on occasion, it *is* possible to find a good used engine.

A friend of mine was broadsided in an intersectional accident a few months ago. The car was less than a year old and she is one of those by-the-book car maintainers. Neither the engine compartment nor the engine was touched in the accident. But the insurance company — as many these days — declared the car totaled: repairing the body damage, which included the car's frame, would simply have run into more money than the company cared to pay. They paid her, as I recall, $3,300 for the car, which they in turn planned to sell as junk.

Yet it is possible that the insurance company would gladly have taken a few hundred dollars for the engine toward recovery of its claim payout.

In a case like that, of course, you've got — once you buy the engine from the insurer — to get a mechanic over there (in this instance, to a dealership's junk-car back lot) to pluck out the engine. It takes some doing. But it can be done. In this example, you'd have bought, without doubt, a good used engine.

Q: Even so, on our engine options list, we'd put the used engine at the bottom?

Thill: For the average driver needing major engine work or an engine replacement, at the bottom.

Q: We still have at least one more major option, when it comes to the engine decision?

Thill: Yes, a 'remanufactured' engine — again, either the whole (long block) or just the bottom power section (short block).

Q: That is your specialty, and that of your company, Motor Machine & Supply, Inc. — 'remanufactured' engines?

Thill: Yes. In remanufacturing — using either an owner's own engine or another just like it — the engine is completely disassembled, piece by piece, part by part, and put through a precision remanufacturing process.

Q: It is, as the name implies, actually remanufactured?

Thill: Totally. Or, if you prefer to call it 'rebuilding,' then remanufacturing is 'factory rebuilding,' as contrasted, say, to what a mechanic does, which might be called 'auto shop rebuilding.'

Q: 'Rebuilding,' but usually with a very considerable difference.

Thill: Usually very considerable, yes.

Remanufacturers, as ourselves, operate a precision engine factory. We have the highly specialized, and very expensive, precision machines and the skilled specialists to operate them, which the average mechanic or garage does not have. Nor do even some of the rebuild specialists, who specialize in rebuilding just one part or another.

Also, we are concerned — because we warrant our remanufactured engines just as do their original manufacturers — with things that few engine rebuild shops can afford to be concerned with: internal engine metallurgy (how a specific rebuilding process may affect a part and its longevity), the effects of torsional stresses — technology that goes to the heart of long engine life.

Q: So, while a remanufactured engine carries that prefix *re,* meaning something other than a brand-new engine, it goes through manufacturing much as it did when it was built. And what emerges is, by nearly any reckoning, a new engine?

Thill: Yes, that is what remanufacturing is all about. Every part, every surface, every orifice of the engine is either replaced with new or brought up to the original manufacturer's specifications. And, frankly, very often better than original.

Q: How can a remanufactured engine be better than the original factory-manufactured new engine?

Thill: Through the use of better, costlier parts — costlier bearings, let's say, rather than the less expensive bearings found in some OEM engines.

It's a matter of economics. The original engine-maker, who may also be the car maker, sets performance standards for every engine part and then goes out to buy them at lowest cost. If what the manufacturer can buy for less meets his engineering specifications, he probably will buy and use the less expensive part.

But, in remanufacturing you have the opportunity, at very little extra cost, of putting in, say, a better bearing — one that not only meets the manufacturer's specifications, but *exceeds* them.

Q: Can a remanufactured engine exceed original specifications in other ways?

Thill: Yes. We are constantly receiving reports of problems that have developed, since their original manufacture, in various engines. Some of these are serious problems that caused whole series of engines to fail prematurely.

In the remanufacturing, we correct these problems.

Q: And after an engine has been remanufactured?

Thill: It is reassembled, often test-run, is sealed in plastic, and is ready for installation, usually by a car owner's own mechanic.

Q: All the mechanic need do, though it takes a bit of doing, is to take out a car owner's old engine and replace it with the remanufactured new one? The mechanic doesn't do — or need to do — anything whatever *internally* within the remanufactured engine?

Thill: Nothing. He connects *externally* what needs to be connected, and the car is ready to run.

Q: For his rebuild money, what does a car owner get when he elects to buy and have installed a remanufactured engine?

Thill: He gets an engine with equal-to-new life expectancy—and, usually, an engine warranted by the remanufacturer for the same number of miles and months as the original factory engine.

Q: Not many mechanics or garages warrant their rebuilds?

Thill: Well, certainly the better mechanics and shops stand behind *their* part of the work. The problem is, and especially on a rebuild involving the complete engine — a long block job — that the mechanic shops out, to specialists, some of the precision work. Most of these specialists are wholly competent. A few may not be. But you can't know for sure, and neither can your mechanic, until a part that one of them furnished *your* mechanic malfunctions in *your* car. By then it is usually too late — perhaps miles and months down the road — to place the blame. So few mechanics or garages can reliably warrant a rebuild.

Q: But aside from the factory-precision job the best of remanufacturers do, there's also the matter of price?

Thill: A published price for every make, model, and year of remanufactured engine, yes.

Q: So, where the car-keeper, handing his engine over to a mechanic for rebuilding, may never know until he gets the bill precisely what the job will cost, the remanufactured engine buyer knows exactly, going in, the rebuilt price of his engine?

Thill: Exactly. Let me read from our current price list. I'll pick an engine at random. Say the Ford 200 cubic-inch straight six-cylinder gasoline engine, with seven main bearings. It's an engine you'll find in some Fords built between 1964 and 1980.

We offer two remanufactured versions of this engine, as for most engines.

You can buy a remanufactured *short block* — just the power-producing lower part — for which our list price is $422, plus a refundable *core charge* of $75. Or you can buy the complete remanufactured engine — the *long block* version of the same engine — for $648, our list price, plus a $130 refundable core charge.

Q: Sounds quite reasonable, except for the core charge thing.

Thill: In today's — or any day's — market, the remanufactured engine is usually quite reasonable and probably considerably less than a mechanic would charge for rebuilding the same engine.

As for those refundable core charges? For most buyers, they don't change the economics at all.

Let me explain. As remanufacturers, we need something to remanufacture — a car owner's old engine or one like it. What generally happens is that the mechanic brings in your engine — which *is* the *core.* So there's no charge. But suppose your engine was stolen, which happens, and you don't have an engine to exchange for the remanufactured one you're buying. Then you pay the core charge.

Q: Suppose a car-keeper, needing a new engine, wants to contact a local engine remanufacturer — either because he's considering a remanufactured engine or just to compare the remanufactured list price with the rebuilt estimate he's got from his mechanic. How does he locate a good, not-too-far-from-home remanufacturer?

Thill: Most remanufacturers, as ourselves, are a bit hard to find. Generally, remanufacturing is a sizable operation, which tends to locate in a town's industrial district.

But they are easy to locate if you contact the industry trade organization to which most of the better remanufacturers belong. Simply write the Automotive Engine Rebuilders Association (AERA), 1238 Waukegan Road, Glenview, Illinois 60024. They'll send you a list of the closest reputable engine remanufacturers.

Q: As I believe you know, when I had my own car rebuilt, what went in was a remanufactured engine. I bought the engine directly from its remanufacturer. Then I hired a mechanic to install it.

Should another major engine rebuild ever become necessary — something I certainly don't foresee — my choice is already made. It would be another remanufactured engine.

RE-ENGINING: HAVE YOU A DIESEL OPTION?

Many car-keepers, facing an engine rebuild or purchase of a remanufactured engine, ponder a logical question: "Why not a diesel instead of my gasoline engine?"

As any logical question, this deserves a logical answer. There is little question that the diesel, by design and by the way it operates, is longer-lived (two to three times longer), sturdier (by necessity, far heftier), and more fuel economical (at least 25 percent more miles per gallon) than a comparable gasoline engine.

A "true" diesel — designed from the outset as a diesel, *not* a gasoline engine remade to act like a diesel — should easily go 200,000 miles, twice the mileage of a gasoline engine, before major overhaul.

Of all engines, the diesel is the longest-lived and most fuel efficient.

Today's mileage champions are steadfastly diesel — with the production car leader, the Volkswagen Diesel Rabbit, pacing the diesel pack with an EPA highway high of 55 miles per gallon. The turbocharged version of the same Rabbit diesel has already, in EPA tests, come close to 70 mpg.

Comparing fuel economy in the same make and model of car, one fitted with a gasoline engine, the other with diesel, is even more convincing.

Dieselizing the Oldsmobile 98, with automatic transmission, raises miles per gallon by fully 50 percent. Doing the same in a Mercedes-Benz, again with automatic transmission, shows upwards of a 56-percent boost in mpg; with the Peugeot, a 47-percent mileage gain when diesel-engined.

Even if diesel fuel were priced the same as gasoline (diesel fuel is cheaper than gasoline, but may not always be), the per-mile fuel cost reduction with diesel is persuasive reason enough for car-keepers to consider a diesel option.

Until just a handful of years ago, however, a switch to diesel — a diesel replacing your present gasoline engine — would likely have proved neither workable nor economic. The reasons were plentiful:

To give anything like comparable gasoline-engined acceleration and get-up-and-go, the diesel that replaces a gas engine must equal the gasoline engine's *combustion size.* That is, if your gasoline engine has a combustion chamber capacity of 250 cubic inches, the diesel that replaces it should have a comparably sized combusion area.

And that was not only expensive — before diesels were sized for the average car — but presented some physical problems as well. So, comparably sized, a diesel was often far larger and heavier dimensionally than the gasoline engine it replaced. In many medium-sized to small cars, a diesel simply would not fit.

But today — and increasingly in the future — a

diesel will fit both physically (dimensionally) and fiscally (economically). Reason: many of today's cars — from the Volkswagen Rabbit to the Mercedes-Benz — are designed for *either* gasoline or diesel, with some changes to accommodate the diesel (a larger radiator, for one).

Moreover, auto makers worldwide for the first time are making diesels designed to fit precisely where their gasoline engines also fit. Thus, the Volkswagen Rabbit may be either gasoline- or diesel-engined, as may many General Motors cars. And GM has just opened a new small-diesel plant that will turn out a new family of small diesels (including V6s) for small to medium-sized GM cars.

What makes the new diesel option even more exciting is *turbocharging.* The turbocharger unit, powered by the diesel's own exhaust gases, forces a huge amount of air into the always air-hungry diesel's combustion chambers. The result: far greater power from the same small diesel — and far better fuel economy.

Turbocharging gives a small, fits-under-your-hood diesel with the power and performance of a same-size gasoline engine, something a nonturbo diesel of comparable gasoline engine size never came close to matching before.

Typically, Mercedes-Benz's 300SD car (powered by a five-cylinder turbocharged Mercedes diesel) is one of the world's great road performers, thanks in large part to its turbo-diesel. The nonturbocharged five-cylinder Mercedes diesel of the same size markedly lacks the turbo's acceleration.

While a diesel-savvy engine mechanic can handle the gasoline-to-diesel trade-out, the acknowledged experts in the field are the so-called *conversion specialists.* For years they have made it their sole business to substitute diesel engines for gasoline engines. In past years many of these conversion experts, even while converting pickup trucks and motor homes from gas to diesel, advised against doing the same with average cars.

Now, with whole new families of small, fuel-misering, turbocharged diesels for the first time becoming available, many conversion specialists are enthusiastically converting average cars to the unaverage turbo-diesel.

A diesel engine costs more, though not all that much more, than a gasoline engine. And some in-car modifications will be necessary to make the diesel a peak performer under your hood.

But the diesel option, only a few years ago iffy at best for average cars, is coming on fast as a viable option for many who intend keeping their cars longer.

Keeping Mechanics Honest
RING AND VALVE JOB: NEED IT OR NOT?

Even if your MSQ (Mechanical Savvy Quotient) is near zero, you can check up on the mechanic while he's checking up on your engine to determine for yourself whether or not you really need the ring and valve job (either or both) he claims you need.

Involved is one of the easiest, quickest, and most revealing of engine health tests: the *compression test.* It generally tells all you really need to know about the efficiency and internal good health, or their lack, of your engine. It also indicates whether the problems — increasing oil use, decreasing power, and gas gulping — are really *internal* to the engine, portending engine repair, or *external,* caused by something outside the engine. Take, for example, the carburetor or the engine's timing, which may require only a little fiddling rather than more expensive repairs.

Almost anyone conversant with engines can make a compression test: a gas station mechanic, engine tune-up man, or garageman.

Here's what's involved. One at a time, or sometimes all at once, the mechanic removes the engine's spark plugs and, into first one spark plug hole and then another, screws in a fitting to a hand-held *compression gauge.* The needle on the gauge shows the *compression* (the force, in pounds per square inch, or *psi*) within the engine cylinder.

Having removed a spark plug and, in its place, attached the compression gauge, the mechanic "turns over the engine": he or an assistant actuates the starter, causing the battery to "crank" the engine, which moves the piston up and down within the cylinder he's testing. For test accuracy, the mechanic tries to crank each cylinder, as he tests it, the same number of times.

On the compression gauge the needle flicks,

reading the compression, in pounds per square inch, within that cylinder. The mechanic moves on to the next spark plug and its spark plug hole, attaches the gauge, and tests that cylinder's compression. He continues this process cranking the engine each time, until he has a compression reading for each cylinder.

Healthy cylinders in gasoline engines should show compression readings between about 150 and 180 pounds per square inch. But engine makers allow considerable leeway. For each engine they make they publish compression specifications, which your mechanic will have. But double-check those figures, just to make sure the mechanic is quoting them correctly and honestly.

Now, if *any* cylinder shows a significant reading *below* this range — say, a reading 40 to 60 pounds below the reading of the other cylinders — there is a problem involving that cylinder. In fact, any reading below 100 pounds per square inch in any cylinder means a cylinder problem.

But, to this point, neither you nor the mechanic can know for sure whether the problem is a *piston ring* (a costlier repair because the piston ring is in the lower part, the *block,* of the engine) or involves a *valve,* which is in the upper part, the *head,* of the engine, where the cure is easier and thus less expensive.

Any mechanic who hands you the verdict "You need a ring *and* valve job," having tested only this far, is plainly dishonest. He doesn't know. What tells him — and you — is one further test, in which the same thing is done but in a different way.

Let's say that, having tested all of the engine's cylinders, your mechanic and you find one with a significantly lower compression reading than the others. *This is the problem cylinder.* And this is the *only* cylinder that needs the second step in the compression test.

Moving to that cylinder, the mechanic again removes its spark plug. This time, however, *before* attaching the compression gauge's hose in the place where the spark plug was, he squirts a little oil directly into the spark plug hole and thus into the suspect cylinder. Now he takes a compression reading as before, cranking the engine over in the process.

If this second reading *improves* (raises) the formerly low compression reading for that cylinder, the problem lies in that cylinder's *piston rings.*

If the second reading shows *no change* from the initial low reading, the problem is *not* in the rings but rather in that cylinder's *valves.*

While there are occasional exceptions to these, as to most other engine tests, they are rare. It is possible, of course, that the *improved* compression reading, indicating a cylinder piston ring problem, masks a valve problem also affecting the same cylinder.

At this point, you face a decision. If that second

Engine valves can very often be adjusted or replaced in the car, and almost always without removing the engine's head.

test (called the *wet test,* by the way, because the cylinder was wetted with oil) showed no compression change, meaning the problem is a *valve,* should you go along with your mechanic's insistence that a ring *and* valve job be done? That is, should you agree to have the rings checked as well as the valves repaired, even though the test did *not* indicate ring trouble but rather a valve problem?

Although high engine mileage and your intention to keep the car can, and may, sway your decision, the dollars-and-sense answer should very probably be "No!"

Tell the mechanic to repair only the valve (a "top engine" — engine *head* — job, relatively easy and not overly costly) and leave it at that. He may argue (as most mechanics will) that while he is "in there," meaning that he has the head off, he might as well put in new rings, even though the compression test indicates you don't need them.

He's not being wholly truthful. He may or may not have to remove the head to fix the valves. In most cases he can repair the valves without ever removing the head as he very well knows but you may not know. But he definitely has to remove the head to reach the rings. And that costs money. Ring replacement is more costly than valve replacement or the grinding of the valve or the *seat* on which the valve operates.

Besides, in doing a valves-only job, he is not "in there" — not really into the engine's body, its cylinder block. He's only, you might say, into its head. The time and costs involved are a little like the choice between hiring a surgeon (ring job) and visiting a shrink (valve job).

While tending to the one valve or its partner, which you now know is faulty, should he repair other valves that seem suspect or worn? Certainly he should. But what about working on the pistons and their rings in the cylinders within the block below the valves? No — not unless the compression test positively indicates a ring problem.

A mechanic who claims he won't guarantee the job unless you tell him to fix the works — rings *and* valves — when fixing the works isn't test-indicated, probably won't stand behind his guarantee anyway. He knows, if you don't, that a problem affecting a single cylinder does not necessarily portend problems with the others. Somewhere down the road, perhaps. But likely not for miles more.

The decision, of course, is yours. The thing to remember is that the compression test seldom lies. Some mechanics do.

Far fewer of them will, however, when you understand what's involved in a ring and valve job and insist that a compression test be made while you watch.

Keeping Mechanics Honest
"BLOWN" GASKET:
DON'T BLOW YOUR TOP

One of the panic words in car-keeping is *gasket.*

The mechanic tells you the car has "blown" a head gasket, a rocker cover gasket, an oil pan gasket, a transmission pan gasket, a thermostat gasket, a valve cover gasket, a timing cover gasket, an intake manifold gasket, an exhaust manifold gasket, or any of a dozen other gaskets.

Somehow, that word *blown* hooked to *gasket* connotes, to some car-keepers, impending doom if not present disaster. They envisage the engine somehow exploding under the hood, the pan and whatever it holds dropping to the garage floor, and the car generally coming apart, if not at the seams, then surely somewhere else, probably at that faulty gasket.

The truth is, if you've ever canned peaches from your backyard, you've handled a gasket — that little rubber sealer between jar glass and lid.

While auto gaskets generally aren't rubber, but rather composition materials, including heat-resistant asbestos and even possibly metal, they are no more complex. Nor are they any more threatening of doom than canning jar gaskets.

What's involved is about the simplest, most quickly fixed, lowest material cost thing that can go wrong with any kept car. Unfortunately, mechanics know only too well that the average owner, conjuring gloom and doom every time he takes the car into an auto shop, is ripe for a little "gasketing" — meaning a padded bill. Nothing pads it easier than a so-called gasket problem.

What do gaskets do? Precisely what they do in canning: they seal something.

In dozens of places in the modern automobile — and in many not all that modern — two pieces of metal come together. One place is atop the engine head, where a metal cover (and sometimes two) fits over the head's valves. Another place is where air is drawn into the engine (the intake manifold), or where spent exhaust gases are discharged (exhaust manifold). Still another place is the pan — the bottom metal piece under the engine's oil reservoir. Yet another place is where the metal casting, into which the radiator's top coolant hose fits, comes together with the engine.

What comes between all of these parts is — you guessed it — a *gasket.*

Were it not for all of these gaskets, your car would leak buckets of oil, gallons of water, and more gasoline than would be safe to leak anywhere. In the case of some areas of the engine, without gaskets your engine would become an acoustical loudmouth; for instance, when a head gasket is "blown," engine noise all but engulfs the car.

In fact, gaskets don't "blow" — not really. Admittedly, some are under extreme pressure from the engine, but most just wear out, heat out, rot out, or are eaten out by various fluids in your car.

Replacing them is a cinch, though you'd seldom guess it from the bill some mechanics hand car-keepers.

Usually, all the mechanic need do is unbolt the two metal parts between which the faulty gasket is sandwiched. He scrapes away or otherwise removes the dead gasket, which by now hardly looks like a gasket at all. In its place, he puts a new gasket, often applying a little adhesive to the gasket or to the metal parts, or to both, to ensure a snug seal. Then he rebolts the pieces together.

Of course, if an oil or transmission pan gasket is in-

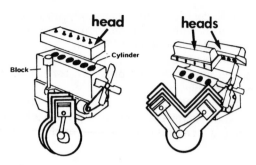

When it comes to gaskets, the V-engine needs two head gaskets because, unlike a "straight" engine, with cylinders in line, the V has two heads. (Drawing courtesy of Caterpillar Tractor Co.)

volved, removing the pan (the bottom of the oil or transmission fluid reservoir) gets a little costlier and dirtier because all the oil or fluid has to be drained out into a container. Once the new gasket and its pan are in place, the mechanic has to refill the engine or transmission (and sometimes the latter's torque converter) with new oil or transmission fluid.

Most mechanics use preholed and preshaped gaskets — very thin, ready-made templates of cork, fiber, asbestos, or other common gasketing materials, designed to go where the old gasket was.

Ready-made gaskets are relatively inexpensive. Should the mechanic make them himself from a sheet of gasket material (few do so nowadays), their cost is piddling.

Ready-made head gaskets — if yours is a V-shaped engine (V6 or V8), you'll likely need two of them because there are two gasketed head covers —

shouldn't cost much more than $4–$6 apiece. That's retail, what the mechanic lists on his bill under materials. Double that for the two that V engines need, and we're talking about material costs of perhaps $8–$12. Add his labor and a bit more for gasket adhesive (sometimes called *gasket compound*). And what have you got? Answer: too often a bill so high you'd imagine those gaskets were made of gold rather than lowly asbestos or corklike material.

In fact, one of the mail order auto supply houses lists, among more than a hundred of them, a complete set of overhaul gaskets for the popular General Motors V8 350 hp engine — a kit containing more than a dozen ready-fit assorted gaskets — for under $15.

The cost of gasket adhesive is even more modest, even for the better universal gasket compound adhesives, which means they work for most gaskets most places in your car.

A four-ounce can, with applicator top (Copper Coat Gasket Compound, to name but one, available at most auto supply stores) retails for a bit under $2. And four ounces, when it comes to gaskets, go a long way.

Gaskets themselves, considering the temperatures, pressures, and corrosive fluids to which they're exposed, likewise go a long way. Eventually, however, most are bound to go. When one does, don't panic. Rather, make very clear to the mechanic that *you* know what a gasket is.

You may be surprised to find that he quotes a job price far lower than you had expected or than he charged you the last time you brought your car in for a gasket job.

Chapter 8: Drive-Train
Revitalizing Get-Up-and-Go

Tow-truckers love drivelines and automatic transmissions. When they go, the towman usually gets a tow. And you face not only what one car owner calls "the psychological embarrassment of being on the hook" (your car hoisted on the hook of the tow truck), but possibly the costliest auto repair: a *transmission overhaul*.

In some cases, an *automatic transmission* that seems to be "out" (it won't manually or automatically shift into gear) is only out of what an automatic transmission can't do without: *transmission fluid*. Or the transmission's filter screen, out of sight and long neglected, may have become so clogged with dirt that it has blocked circulation of transmission fluid, causing the transmission to slip, failing to shift into a gear or, when shifted into one gear, slipping into another. Or it might as easily be the valve

Drive train transmits the engine's power to the wheels: (2) automatic transmission filter needs regular servicing; (3) modulator, vacuum operated from engine, assures smooth shifting; (4) clutch (in manual-shift cars) connects and disconnects engine from the drive train. (Drawing courtesy of Fram Corporation.)

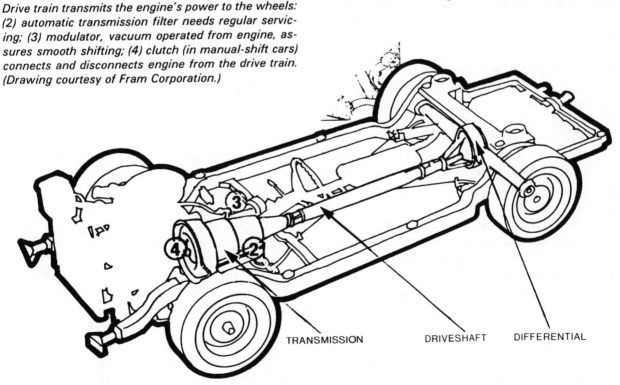

TRANSMISSION   DRIVESHAFT   DIFFERENTIAL

Transmission's pan looks precisely as you might expect: a pan. Pan is removed when transmission is serviced.

(on most cars except Chrysler products) that receives vacuum "signals" from the engine. The valve, its hose, or other parts may be clogged or leaking. Or it could, of course, be what most car-keepers would like to avoid: an ailment cured only by a transmission rebuild.

What about the *driveline*, also called the *propeller shaft* on rear-wheel-powered cars? If it should break, none of the engine's power reaches the wheels. And you're stopped. Yet it is possible that a little lubrication in the right spots, during the car's routine oil change and lubrication, would have prevented the driveline from breaking.

What the transmission, whether *manual* or *automatic*, and the driveline are all about is the transfer of the engine's power to the wheels. The transmission also controls that power so your car doesn't take off like a missile.

Typically, when an engine is producing its *rated* (highest) *power*, its crankshaft is turning at incredible speed—in some engines, well above 5,000 revolutions per minute. If the crankshaft directly drove a car's wheels, the wheels would turn at the same speed as the engine—5,000 revolutions per minute. And a car would quite literally rocket down the highway.

What prevents it is the transmission. Its *gearing* reduces the crankshaft's output speed to manageable speed. And, whether automatically or manually, it gives you control over the speed.

Thus, no matter how fast the engine's crankshaft is turning, the car's wheels turn only a fraction as fast. In fact, when the transmission is in *neutral*, the crankshaft can be turning 5,000 revolutions per minute, even 6,000 rpm, and the wheels aren't turning at all.

Once the transmission's gearing has reduced the engine's output speed by various amounts—depending whether you are in first (the gearing's greatest reduction), second, third, or fourth gear, or higher for some transmissions, the transmission transmits this now reduced engine speed to the rear wheels by means of the driveline. Turning at the gear-reduced speed, the driveline turns the gearing in the *differential,* housed in the gear case, which is part of the *rear axle,* turning the wheels. All of this speed-reducing gearing, including the transmission and its driveline, are called the *drive train,* because they comprise a series of moving parts that drive the wheels.

Front-wheel drive cars don't have or need a driveline as long as for rear-wheel-driven cars, but they have something similar. It is far shorter and is part of the *transaxle* that powers the car's front wheels.

Transmissions are designed, given proper use and care, to last the life of the engine—100,000 miles or more. The problem is that many car-keepers neglect to give their automatic transmissions what every other moving part of a car routinely gets: regular maintenance. For most automatic transmissions, this should mean a *transmission servicing* every 12,000–15,000 miles—roughly, once a year if your mileage is average.

Transmission servicing—by a transmission specialist—is quick, relatively inexpensive (the cost is usually less than for an engine tune-up), and vital.

Without regular servicing, an automatic transmission may well need a costly overhaul at 30,000–50,000 miles, instead of going without major rework twice to three times that long.

In the servicing, the old transmission fluid, which wears out in time, is replaced.

The transmission's easily dirt-clogged filter screen is cleaned or replaced. Various other transmission parts are checked, including the cooling hoses. The whole job seldom takes longer than 45 minutes. Sometimes it can be done while you wait.

Your wait for the tow truck, by contrast, should be a time for calculated strategy, not panic.

Where shall you tell the towman to tow you? If you've had the transmission regularly serviced by a transmission specialist, his shop is obviously the place to be towed. If he is honest and knows you car and its transmission, you may get off the hook (his and the towman's) with only a little transmission fiddling. Maybe, you can get by with just the cost of a few pints of transmission fluid.

If you don't know a transmission place, and most drivers in that predicament don't, it is far better *not* to call a tow truck until, from the nearest phone, you (1) ask friends who have had transmission work to recommend a specialist, and (2) call a few transmission repair places to get their quick diagnosis and estimate of what the work may cost.

One thing you must be wary of: some towmen, unless you tell them where you want to be towed, will haul you to a garage or transmission shop that pays them a commission for towing in business. In the end, you pay—with a far higher than normal repair bill. And for work that is too often lower in quality than most.

What, though, of local independent transmission shops and the advertised franchised transmission places?

Here is an appraisal, based on transmission shop surveys:

- Of two equally competent transmission specialty places, the franchised one will likely charge more for the same job than will an independent. The "more" may run to $100–$200. But the chain outfit's warranty for its work, if it gives one, and most do, is apt to be more solid than an independent's.

- Given the choice of two unknown repair places, pick the franchised one. Should its work prove faulty, you can take your complaint to the parent company—usually a major corporation with a setup to deal with complaints and with franchisees who botch or overcharge for their jobs.

- *But* you will likely get the best work at the lowest price from a local, competent, in-business-for-himself transmission specialist. He earns his living from referrals from friends and neighbors and from *their* friends and neighbors.

YEARS-LONGER STRATEGY: AUTOMATIC TRANSMISSION

1. Every time you have the engine's oil checked, have the fluid level of the transmission checked.
2. If the transmission needs more fluid, make sure that what the station attendant puts in is a good grade transmission fluid.
3. About once a year — every 12,000-15,000 miles — have the transmission serviced, preferably by a transmission specialist.

SYMPTOMS/CAUSES: AUTOMATIC TRANSMISSION

Symptom	Possible Cause
Slips out of gear	Low transmission fluid or more serious problem
No "up-shift" (stays in low gear)	Engine vacuum problem (except in Chrysler products) or more serious transmission problem
Car won't go	Low transmission fluid, clogged transmission filter, or more serious problem
Tends to slip into second gear (especially some Ford products)	Needs fresh transmission fluid
Lags or hesitates in shifting, particularly when engine and transmission are cold	Loss of internal transmission hydraulic pressure; onset of transmission rebuild
Transmission oil smells burnt (especially after short, hot-weather drive or when pulling a trailer)	Transmission running too hot; needs fresh transmission fluid
Clattering sound when you first start out	Transmission fluid low or more serious problem

Chapter 9: Suspension System
Smoothing the Ride

What suspends your car—cushions and controls the ride—are a lot of familiar words and some that may not be familiar at all:

Leaf Springs. These suspend the car's body over the rear axle.

Coil Springs. These may work in partnership with the leaf springs in back and with the *front suspension* and steering components in front.

Upper and *Lower Control Arms.* In the steering-suspension systems, these allow the front wheels to move up and down over bumps.

Engine Mounts. These are not properly suspension components, but they hold the engine fixed in place.

The suspension system, which mates body to wheels, the body suspended above the frame by springs, shock absorbers, and parts of the steering system: (1) coil springs (though leaf springs are more common. Also used are torsion bars); (2) shock absorbers; (3) control arms, in the steering system, permit wheels to raise and lower over bumps. (Drawing courtesy of Fram Corporation.)

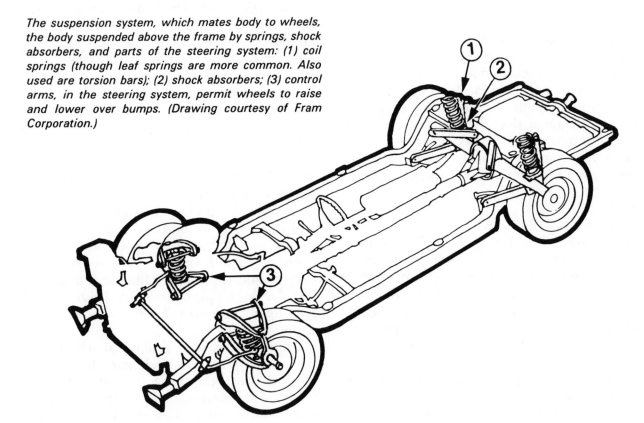

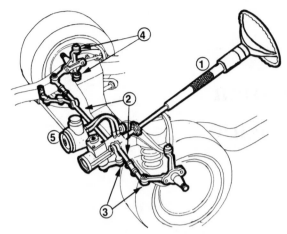

In the steering system are a lot of familiar words used by mechanics in trying to explain what's wrong: (1) steering column; (2) linkage; (3) grease fittings; (4) ball joints; (5) power-steering unit. (Drawing courtesy of Fram Corporation.)

Ball Joints. These are the critical pivot-point links between the front wheels and the steering system, whose loss, through excessive wear and breakage, can make steering difficult or cause you to lose control of the car.

Shock Absorbers. This term is the most familiar of all.

Where shock absorbers are concerned, many otherwise healthy station attendants and mechanics come down with a sudden case of shock absorbitis. What cures shock absorbitis is money—yours. As part of the cure, you agree that the mechanic should install a pair of new shock absorbers, front or rear, or four new shocks all around. But does your kept car really need new shock absorbers? And if so, where and how many?

There's one quick way to tell—the way mechanics often test for tired or faulty shocks. Give your car the *bounce test:* With the car on a firm, level surface (any normal street will do), make a tour of the car, stopping at each of its four corners. At each corner, vigorously and repeatedly (four to six times) push down on the corner until it begins to bounce up and down. Finally, give the bouncing corner one last vigorous downward push and see what happens. If the car corner continues to bounce more

than *twice,* the shock absorber that is supposed to steady that corner needs to be replaced (shock absorbers usually cannot be repaired).

If the bounce test shows up only one bad shock, two will still have to be replaced (either rears or fronts), since shock replacement, to do the job right, is always done in pairs.

Bounce testing for shocks, you've also demonstrated what shocks do: they *damp* (limit) the up-and-down bouncing of the car's body on its springs. Without shocks, or with nonoperating ones, the ride can be bouncy and, in extreme cases, potentially dangerous.

There are other ways to check for shocks that have lost their ability to damp the bounce or to reduce side movement (sway) of a car. A shock leaking its hydraulic fluid, which is the working fluid of the shocks, probably needs to be replaced.

Shock absorbers on the majority of cars, however, as well as the newer McPherson struts on some late-model American and many imported cars, do other things than smooth the ride. They also prevent a car from "bottoming"—overreaching its springs and coming down hard when hitting a pot-hole or running over railroad tracks. And they prevent a car from nose-diving during sudden emergency braking.

Driving with worn or poor shocks, while sometimes causing handling problems, is something a lot of car-keepers do every day, unaware that they have a shock problem, if in fact they do, until a mechanic suggests new shocks.

Are shocks really all that critical? Yes and no. For around-town driving, you hardly notice whether your shocks are good or bad. Having new ones installed only occasionally gives the car a new feel. But for high-speed highway driving, fast turning, or rough-road going, the answer is definitely yes.

Another reason to replace shocks is tire wear. Faulty shocks tend characteristically to wear tires—the characteristic being little nearly circular wear places in the treads. And really bad shocks shove more of the

Cimarron, Cadillac's new small car, has (1) McPherson strut suspension up front; (2) valve-adjustable shock absorbers in rear; (3) a 19 mm rear stabilizer bar; and (4) a 28 mm front stabilizer bar—a suspension car's maker says gives it a far better than usual small car ride. (Photo courtesy of Cadillac Division General Motors Corp.)

load and more road work onto the springs.

Shock replacement itself is generally easy and quick (45–60 minutes does it even when replacing all four). While *standard* replacement shocks, built to the same specifications as the original factory-installed ones, are all right, and should last with normal driving, an average of 25,000 miles or so, the *heavy-duty* type lasts longer and may give a car a firmer, less bouncy ride.

There are also *spring-assisted* shocks, a heavy-duty type designed for cars with heavy engines or which carry heavy loads. And for on-again, off-again superloads—as when you hitch on a trailer—you might need *air adjustable shocks*, whose load-carrying ability can be varied with the weight of the load.

The newer *McPherson* struts are another story—costlier and more difficult to replace but also generally lighter in weight and more compact than standard shocks. And,

as such, they act somewhat as aids to fuel economy. That's why weight-conscious car designers use them and will probably use them more often in the future. Virtually all of the new front-wheel drive models, with their engines up front, have McPherson struts up front.

One problem (among many) with the McPhersons is that the way the front pair is installed prevents the wheels from being

McPherson strut, now found in many front-wheel drive cars, is both shock absorber and spring—and an integral part of both suspension and steering systems. (Drawing courtesy of Fram Corporation.)

aligned normally. The struts, in effect, take over some of the alignment chores.

What's good is that *normal* alignment involves a smaller task and may cost less.

What's bad is that *abnormal* front-end alignment problems—involving more than simple adjustments—often indicate a strut problem and, as often, the replacement of strut parts or of the strut itself.

In a doleful (for car-keepers) analysis of the two, a recent American Automobile Association wrap-up said this:

"The McPherson-type shock absorber costs up to *four* times as much to replace as a conventional shock absorber. The labor time to install the strut can be up to *three* times more than installing regular shock absorbers."

If your car doesn't have the McPhersons be thankful.

But suppose, as is all but inevitable for most cars, and certainly for the kept car, that a station attendant or mechanic recommends new shocks or McPhersons. Do you say, "All right, go ahead and install them?"

No, you don't. Most especially you don't if, as any car-keeper with an eye on the miles ahead and a mind geared to getting the most from every maintenance dollar, you've been following your strategy schedule. With shocks due for replacement every 25,000 miles or so, it's one of those recurring expenses you wish you could eliminate. And you can—but not by having shocks installed at just any service station or garage.

In one of those fairly rare cases (which also includes *mufflers*) in which patronizing a franchise shop is the way to go, you go straight to the likes of a Midas Muffler (or similar) franchised place. The franchise shops (including Midas) warrant replacement of shock absorbers at no further (or future) charge either for parts or labor for the life of the car. Replace shocks once, and you never pay again for new.

The franchise places' guarantee on the McPhersons is more limited, but still apt to be the best deal in town. Depending on franchise policy, McPherson struts (the strut part) may be warranted to 50,000 miles; you pay only the cost of the labor. Replacement of the strut's cartridge, for domestic cars, may carry a full 50,000 mile warranty—no charge for replacement. Rarely can or do less specialized shops match the replacement warranties of the franchised shock and muffler places.

What, then, restores the ride should it noticeably need it? Principally four things:

The springs, which give only occasional trouble. (If badly overloaded by too much weight for too long—your car's not a truck—or by excessive mileage, a leaf spring's leaves can break.)

The shock absorbers, whether the conventional or the McPherson type.

The front-end suspension-steering sytem whose alignment, as well as the alignment of the wheels, is critical to ride, as is the condition of the steering system components.

The tires—their type (whether bias ply or radial), balance, width, and inflation pressures all contributing to how well or poorly a car rides.

With these four routinely in order, and righted when wrong, a kept car will ride easier—and usually as smoothly as when fresh from the factory.

Chapter 10: Wheels, Tires, and Brakes
Renewing Road Fitness

What brand-new product can't be satisfactorily used until it has been repaired? The answer is the tires.

With few exceptions, the tires you buy are out-of-round or out-of-weight (the rubber heavier in one place than another). To correct these unavoidable manufacturing flaws, tires have to be *balanced*, either by hand (*hand-balanced*) or by rotation at high speed on a balancing machine (*spin-balanced*).

Either way—the spin balance being by far the more accurate—the tire man adds little lead weights around the wheel's circumference. While not strictly repairs, they correct the tire/wheel imbalance.

One tire maintenance "do" that's seldom listed is keeping check on your *wheel weights*. They sometimes come off. When they do, the tire is no longer balanced. An out-of-balance front tire, especially, not only has short wear life (as does any unbalanced tire), but throws the front end and steering out of balance. And the car handles poorly.

An easy way to keep track of wheel weights is to number each with an indelible-ink marker. Then jot down the number of weights on each wheel. If, when checking, you discover that a wheel that's supposed to have five weights has only four—or if a numbered weight is missing—you know at a glance that that wheel is no longer in balance. Waiting for the imbalance to show up in tread wear can cost you 10,000 miles of tire life.

For car-keepers, the tire decision—when, how many, and what tires to buy, how to maintain them, and whether, when buying new, to have a front-end alignment done—seems to be among the simplest of driver decisions. Actually, it is not that easy at all.

What helps to make it otherwise is that few car-keepers understand how important, aside from safety, tires are to a car's performance.

Slightly underinflated tires improve the ride but reduce fuel economy. Overinflated tires help fuel economy and roughen the ride. You can't have both.

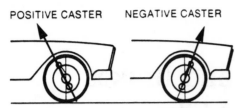

POSITIVE CASTER   NEGATIVE CASTER

In wheel alignment, caster is the forward or backward tilt of the wheel to help wheel return to straight-ahead position after a turn. (Drawing courtesy of Fram Corporation.)

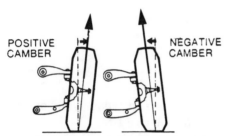

POSITIVE CAMBER   NEGATIVE CAMBER

Camber, in wheel alignment, is the inward or outward tilt of the wheel, so that wheel, when in motion, will keep its tread ideally flat on the pavement. (Drawing courtesy of Fram Corporation.)

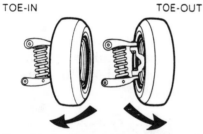

TOE-IN   TOE-OUT

Toe-in, in wheel alignment, usually sets wheels slightly pigeon-toed, although they may also be set to toe-out. Aim is to keep wheels parallel when car is in motion. (Drawing courtesy of Fram Corporation.)

Wrong-width tires up front, on cars not designed for them, can cause the front wheels to shimmy and the car to shake.

Overinflated tires can undo all the soft-ride good works of springs and shock absorbers and make the ride a teeth rattler. Nonetheless, overinflation—say five to seven pounds above the normal recommendation—improves fuel economy noticeably while just as noticeably de-comforting the ride. It is axiomatic that you can't have maximum ride comfort and maximum fuel economy, too.

Underinflated tires can give you a straight-from-the-factory soft ride but cut tire life in half and cost you an extra few miles per gallon or so in fuel economy.

And mismatched treads—front tires with dissimilar wear—can cause the car to pull left or right when you brake, making you think you need a brake job when all you really need is a tire job (new tires up front).

Making your decision no easier is the jargon of tires, wheels, and brakes. When a mechanic says you need "new brakes," he probably means you need new *linings*, in the case of *drum-type brakes*, or new *pads*, if they're *disc-type brakes*. And when he recommends a "wheel alignment," he actually means he intends to "misalign" the wheels to bring them into alignment. What's involved are the usual three main adjustments that constitute *front-end alignment*—the adjustment of each front wheel's *caster, camber,* and *toe-in*.

Caster is a wheel's tilt forward (*negative caster*) or backward (*positive caster*) from the vertical.

Most wheels are set with positive caster, or a backward tilt, which helps wheels and tires track properly on the pavement and return to straight-ahead position after a turn. Too great a caster angle makes a manually steered car hard to steer and a power-steered one road-wander at high speed and shimmy at low speed.

Camber is a wheel's outward or inward tilt—thus its angle—from the vertical. If a wheel is set to tilt outward it has *positive camber*; if tilted inward, *negative camber*.

While caster has more to do with steering and how a car handles, camber has more effect on tire wear. Camber seeks to give a tire maximum contact with the road—keep its tread flat on the pavement—when the car is in motion. Too much positive (outward) tilt wears the outside shoulder of front tires. Too much inward (negative) tilt wears a tire's inside shoulder.

Toe-in, as its name implies, aims to set the wheels slightly pigeon-toed to keep them parallel when the car is in motion. The wheels otherwise tend to spread out and end up something less than parallel.

Too much toe-in causes tires to scuff the pavement, causing little featherlike wear marks on their treads.

And there you have it—the demystification of front-wheel alignment, in which the wheels are actually misaligned (tilted backward, outward, or toed in) so that when in motion they are road-aligned.

Accomplishing this wheel-corrective sleight of hand requires relatively expensive equipment (costing from a few thousand dollars to $10,000 or so) and considerable skill and painstaking work. Just any mechanic can't properly align wheels. And no mechanic can without the necessary equipment, which includes an *alignment rack*. Still, the usual cost for front-end alignment isn't high.

Places that specialize in tires not only have the equipment and the practice, but, certainly more than shops less specialized, the knowledge to do the job right.

If, by your strategy schedule, you buy new tires all around (a set of four) whenever the time comes to buy new, a front-end alignment (also called a wheel alignment) is self-insurance against wear-shortening the lives of your new treads. At other times, when you're replacing only a tire or two (though paired replacement is always preferred), front-end alignment is iffy. But, *if* the front tires you're replacing show telltale tread wear (see "Symptoms/Causes: Tire Wear," page 89), you have no choice: have the wheels aligned.

You can avoid unnecessary alignment jobs by avoiding hitting curbs, which throw alignment out, going too fast over those pavement planted slow-barriers in some parking lots, or, with power steering, forcing wheels against a curb to the steering-squealing point when getting into or out of a tight parking space.

In older kept cars, not properly kept up, worn steering or suspension system components can throw the front wheels out of alignment or make it difficult to hold alignment once it is set.

And, no doubt about it, everything aligns better, rolls better, and rides better if, when you buy them, you buy them all at once—four new tires at a crack.

And now the considerably-more-than-$64 question: Does it really make sense, granted even their longer life and aid to fuel economy, to buy the more expensive *radials* rather than the less costly *bias* type of tires?

Car-keeping's strategy schedule, and its pay-as-you-drive hypothetical $100-a-month budget, suggests that, of two products comparable in quality and appearance, the car-keeper would find it easier budgeting (and paying) for the less expensive.

Their makers' statements to the contrary, the radial and bias are comparable in appearance, quality, and less generally known, in cost-per-mile to use. The chief difference is that a set of the bias ply, at say $40 a tire, costs $160 or so, while a set of the radial, at $70 or so apiece, costs $280. Buying bias takes about 1½ months of car-keeper budget; the radial, more than 2½ months. Yet their *per-mile cost* per set is all but identical, with a slight cost advantage going to the bias.

You can figure this yourself. That $160 set of the bias, though perhaps handing you only 25,000 tread miles, costs only .0064¢ per mile to run on. A set of $280 radials, good for perhaps 40,000 miles, calculates out to a tread-mile cost of .0070¢ a mile—or a cost-per-mile standoff with the bias.

And, though radials have less rolling resistance than the bias ply (thus the radial's boost to fuel economy), and give better

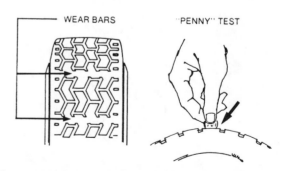

Penny test for tire wear (when tires do not have built-in wear bars): Insert Lincoln head penny head down into tire grooves. If, in any groove, you can see all of Lincoln's head, tire needs replacement. (Drawing courtesy of Fram Corporation.)

traction in snow (but still nowhere as good as either studded tires or plain old-fashioned tire chains), they have generally been overtouted.

Besides, there are some advantages to retiring every 25,000 miles or so, rather than at the radial's longer 40,000-mile mark.

With air pollution in some areas aging tire casings faster, and many drivers curb-damaging their sidewalls, to say nothing of scuffing whitewalls, a radial's tread may look peachy-keen while its sidewalls (especially the whitewalled ones) look anything but.

Two years and maybe 24,000 miles into your radials, but with still a year to go, a friend is likely to exclaim, "You've really curb-whacked the looks out of those white sidewalls." And what are you going to say? "I know, but the treads look good." Only the tire man ever looks at your treads.

With the bias's lower run-mileage, you get a spanking new set of tires every couple of years, at a smidgeon *less* cost per mile than running radials. And their strategy schedule budgeting is far easier.

What can sabotage your strategy, however, is failing to *rotate* your tires so as to

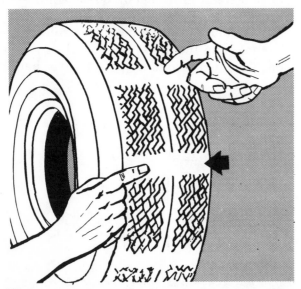

When wear bars show in tire tread, it's time to replace the tire. Bars are now required in all new tires by federal law. (Drawing courtesy of Tire Industry Safety Council.)

give them all about equal wear. That way, wearing evenly, they'll all be ready for replacements at once—and you'll be ready for four new.

Rotation—at the *least* at the midway point of tire life (12,000 miles for the bias, 20,000 miles for the radials, but better even more often)—also can add bonus mileage to treads.

The *rotation pattern* (how the tires are traded around the wheels) for the bias and radial differ and sometimes from one tire brand to another.

Generally, however, and assuming you don't have a spare (as today, many new cars don't), the bias's *X-pattern* for rotation switches the tires diagonally: the front left to the right rear, the front right to the rear left. In radial *H-pattern* rotation, front tires merely trade places with their corresponding rears.

It goes without saying, because it's been said so often before, that the radial and bias ply (including belted or other versions of both) don't mix on the same car. Go with either the radial or the bias, but not with both.

But with the new front-wheel drive, radial-tired cars, all of this nice rotational theory and tread-stretching practice may go out the window—at least that's what several recent studies indicate. They show, for these cars and their radials, that if you don't rotate at all, but just buy new fronts, the rears can go as long as 90,000 miles.

Unfortunately for car-keepers, whatever your car, your *brakes* can't. For most brakes, 25,000 miles or so is about it. And for some—again those front-wheel drive, radial-running new models with their engines up front—it's a lot less. If, a paragraph or so ago, car-keepers driving the front-engined new models were celebrating because they might get up to 90,000 miles on their rear treads, the celebration is over. Those same heavy-in-front (because that's where the engine is) new models can go through a set of front-end disc brakes in less than 10,000 miles.

Is there anything you can do, as a driver and car-keeper, to extend brake life, whether you car's brake expectancy is 25,000 miles or something less?

Two things.

First, you can drive "ahead"—your mind and attention on the road situation *ahead* so you're never forced to panic-brake, the kind of hard braking that can cut brake life expectancy in half.

And you can come to know enough about brakes, whatever their type, to get done what may have to be done to extend, at lower cost, their life and mileage.

The first step is understanding how brakes work.

On *drum-type brakes*, the round brake drum, rotating with the wheel, turns around two semicircular *brake shoes* to which are mounted (usually with rivets) the *brake linings*, most of them a heat-resistant composite of asbestos. Apply the brakes and, by hydraulic pressure (*brake fluid*), the shoes and their linings are forced *outward* to contact and slow, or stop, the drum and thus the wheel and the car.

On *disc-type brakes*, a metal *disc* (the rotor) turns between a set of *pads* (brake linings), one pad on each side of the disc. When you apply the brakes, a hydraulically powered *caliper*, which resembles a powerful pair of fingers, squeezes the pads *inward* against the rotating disc, slowing or stopping it and the car.

Disc brakes grew up in Europe where race cars, among others, have had them for years. The disc has some special advantages over the drum type.

Disc braking is more consistent and dependable. Disc brakes aren't as prone to fading (losing braking efficiency when hot) as the drum type. Wetting doesn't affect the disc's braking (drive through curb-deep water with drum brakes and you'll often discover you're brakeless). That doesn't happen with disc brakes. And replacing the disc's pads, their linings, is a snap.

Both types suffer from modernization, which can cost you money. Self-adjusting features in both no longer give pedal warning when the brake linings need replacement. In the old days, when linings were worn, the brake pedal sank to the floor-

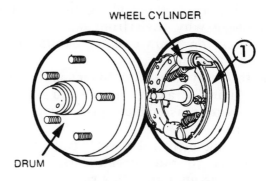

DRUM BRAKE ASSEMBLY

Drum-type brakes operate by hydraulically (through means of brake fluid) forcing a pair of semicircular brake shoes, to which brake lining (1) is attached, outward to contact wheel's drum, which turns with wheel around the brakes. Critical wheel cylinder, which controls hydraulic pressure, should by rebuilt when brakes are relined. (Drawing courtesy of Fram Corporation.)

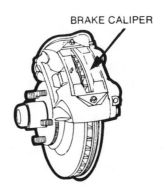

DISC BRAKE ASSEMBLY

In disc-type brakes, powerful fingerlike caliper hydraulically squeezes disc pads, one on either side of revolving disc, against disc to apply brakes. (Drawing courtesy of Fram Corporation.)

board. Today, the linings can be shot and your brake pedal remains perky and normal.

Usually, the first time you are aware of bad linings is when you hear a metallic grinding when you brake. By then it's usually too late for a quick, inexpensive brake relining or disc repadding.

Canny car-keepers do the recommended: have brakes inspected every 10,000 miles. And that's *mandatory* if your car is a front-wheel drive with the engine in front. On these heavy-in-front models the front disc brakes do virtually all of the car's braking, with the rears going along for the ride, explaining why their front discs may go, depending on your braking habits, in as few as 7,000 miles.

With everybody and his cousin seemingly "doing" brakes, how can you get them redone with reasonable expectancy of long-wear life?

Shopping out brake work calls for the car-keeper to put on blinders, ignoring those come-on bait ads promising something for almost nothing: new brakes all around for scarcely more than the price of a new bias ply tire.

What they usually hand you is shoddy work, shoddier linings, and, inevitably, a bill that bears no resemblance to the advertised price. Nor is "brake-baiting" confined to the shady or no-name places. Brake work is big business, and big businesses (chain department stores with auto shops as well as some big-brand tire stores) brake-bait as often as the small.

The brake shop you're looking for takes the time to give attention to details. And, while not cut-rate, it gives you honest return for what it charges.

The attention involves rebuilding some brake parts, greasing others, and bringing the *entire* brake, not just its obviously worn linings or pads, up to maximum brake-life expectancy. Many shops don't come close to doing that.

The honesty concerns the quality of brake linings or disc pads you get. Some brake linings are good for 25,000–35,000 miles, some for 15,000, and others for 10,000. And some are good for nothing. Not even many experts can tell the difference simply by inspecting a sample of lining.

For car-keepers there's only one shop-out solution. Find a super brake specialist—invariably a small, independent honest john who is also expert at what he does—and stick with him.

Even so, if you have drum-type brakes, always *insist* (although the super places do it routinely) that the *wheel cylinders,* the hydraulic piston heart of drum brakes, be *rebuilt,* a simple but essential job. While he's got the wheel off anyway, he should *repack* the *wheel bearings*—an expensive-sounding phrase for doing nothing more than smearing fresh grease on the wheel bearings. If he's a slowpoke, that repacking job might just take 30 seconds.

Attention to your brakes—as attention to tires, to wheels, and to their alignment—goes a long way toward renewing any kept car's road fitness.

SYMPTOMS/CAUSES: BRAKES

Symptom	Possible Cause
Dashboard brake light stays on	1. Brake fluid leak or lack of fluid 2. Brake master cylinder problem (*Do not drive* in either case.)
Pedal goes to floor	1. Brake fluid leak or fluid extremely low 2. Brake linings or pads badly worn or out of adjustment 3. Brake master cylinder problem (*If you must drive to brake shop,* use caution.)
Pedal is spongy (pumping pedal partially restores brakes)	1. Brake linings/pads worn 2. Air in brake hydraulic system 3. Brake fluid level low

Symptom	Possible Cause
Metallic scraping sound when brakes applied	1. Brake linings or pads badly worn
Car pulls left or right when you brake	1. Brake linings or pads unevenly worn 2. Contamination, such as dirt, water, or grease on linings or pads 3. Front-end suspension or wheel alignment problem 4. Brake fluid leak
Uneven front-to-rear brake action (rears grab)	1. Brake fluid leak 2. Air trapped in system 3. Worn rear brake linings 4. Brake system problem 5. Tire pressure incorrect 6. Driver "riding" brakes
Brakes squeal or squeak when applied	1. Brake linings worn 2. Dust on brake linings 3. Drum or disc problem 4. Brake-shoe guides need lubrication
Brakes clatter when applied	1. Brake linings or pads not making proper contact with brake drum or disc
Brake response lags	1. Wet or greasy brake lining 2. Brake fluid contaminated or improper 3. Brake system problem

Symptoms/Causes: Steering

Symptom	Possible Cause
(power-steered cars) Steers hard	1. Tire inflation low, uneven 2. Front-end alignment faulty 3. Power steering failing 4. Steering gear adjustment too tight
(manually-steered cars) Steers hard	1. Tire inflation low, uneven 2. Front-end alignment faulty 3. Steering gear and front-end suspension's ball joints need lubrication
(power-steered cars) Screeching noise when wheel turned hard in either direction	1. Power steering's drive belt loose or worn 2. Power steering fluid low

Symptom	**Possible Cause**
Steering wheel and front end vibrate at high speed	1. Tires/wheels out of balance 2. Wheels/front end out of alignment
Car pulls to left or right while cruising	1. One front tire underinflated or going flat 2. Front wheels misaligned 3. In sudden cold weather, one tire may be only partially inflated
Car pulls to left or right when braking	1. Front brakes faulty, worn 2. Front tires underinflated or misinflated
(front-wheel drive cars) Steering wheel moves back and forth when you make slow turns	1. Front-wheel drive shafts need lubrication or repair/overhaul

Telltale tire wear indicates incorrect tire inflation, misalignment of wheels, tires out of balance, or neglect of suspension or steering systems. (Photos courtesy of Tire Industry Safety Council.)

SYMPTOMS/CAUSES: TIRE WEAR
(Tread Wear)

Symptom	Possible Cause
Wear in patches	1. Tire(s) out of balance or wheel rim bent
Wear down middle of tread	1. Tire overinflated
Wear excessive on both sides	1. Tire underinflated
Wear excessive on one shoulder or the other	1. Alignment problem; wheel's camber incorrect
Wear in feathered pattern	1. Alignment problem; toe-in setting incorrect
Circular wear spots	1. Suspension system problem; probably faulty shock absorbers

Chapter 11: Radiator, Hoses, and Belts
Stopping Leaks and Squeaks

In the strategy of car-keeping you can sometimes let the radiator go—but *not* its leaks.

There's a difference. Rather than replace a leaky radiator with new, it can be *doctored* with store-bought gunk (the so-called liquid or powdered "leak stoppers"), but use them gingerly. It can also be *patched, reworked,* and even its high-pressure cap *replaced* with one of lower pressure, relieving the radiator's inner pressure and hopefully stopping its leaks.

What about radiator *replacement*—the purchase and installation of a *new* radiator? *That* can often be put off for months, even years. But serious radiator and coolant system leaks—whether from the *radiator* itself, its *hoses,* the *water pump* or the *thermostat well* through which radiator coolant flows—can't be put off at all. Even a "little" leak quickly reduces the total amount of coolant in the radiator and its distribution system. And radiator temperature—thus engine temperature—begins to soar. Too soon, the car is boiling.

Keeping coolant to prescribed levels in today's newer cars is doubly important, especially in small cars. Today's four- and six-cylinder small-car, high-speed engines work harder and faster than the larger, relatively slower-going eight-cylinder engines. Auto makers, to reduce overall weight, which is especially critical in small-car performance and fuel economy, have reduced radiator size and capacity to a point where, if the radiator isn't operating right, it's operating wrong.

In nearly all of today's lighter-weight, fuel-economy cars—whatever their size—there is scarcely any longer a margin for error when it concerns the radiator. Any leak, no matter how small, puts a small car's already undersized (for its job) cooling system in jeopardy.

Those "overflow recovery" containers, which now come on some new cars and are popular add-ons, are designed with more in mind than their advertised reason for being: to catch and recover expensive coolant that ordinarily might be vented and wasted

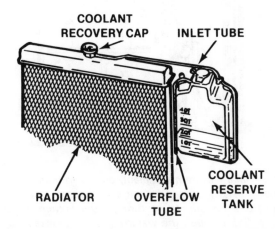

Besides recovering coolant, which might otherwise be vented (from overflow tube), reserve tank helps keep coolant at proper level. (Drawing courtesy of McQuay-Norris, Inc.)

through the radiator's *overflow tube*. The better reason for adding an overflow recovery container, which plugs into the overflow tube, creating a closed coolant circuit, is to *add radiator cooling capacity not built into it by the car's maker.*

That's right, $10,000 and more expensive new models now come equipped with overflow canisters because they're cheaper than building the radiator right—with the capacity it should have had in the first place.

With due respect to the late Walt Disney, it is all pretty Mickey Mouse. But, then, many newer car things are even mousier.

Still, whether it cools a big engine or a small one, there's nothing all that complex about your car's cooling system and its radiator. So let's—in plotting car-keeping strategy—take a quick look at the radiator and its system.

Your car's radiator, either positioned up front so the wind can breeze through it or, if in back, likewise fed a windstream, has a single-minded job: to rid the engine of about one-third of the heat it produces. Another third of the engine's heat goes out the exhaust. A final third is converted to power to drive the wheels.

Since heat is energy and energy is power,

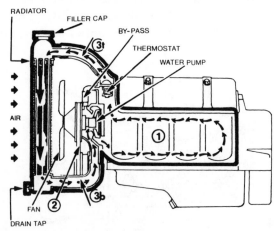

The coolant system's coolant, cooled through the radiator, exits (pumped by the water pump) out of the radiator's bottom, flows through the bottom radiator hose (3b), through the water pump, and makes a loop through the engine (1), then flows back, en route once again to the radiator, past the thermostat and into the radiator's top hose (3t). (Drawing courtesy of Fram Corporation.)

these rough—but basically accurate—heat-use figures tell you something about the automobile's efficiency. It isn't all that great, not if it can put to power—at the wheels—only about one-third of all the heat energy it creates. And many cars are not even that efficient.

In doing that critical one-third of engine cooling, the radiator system is a closed loop, meaning that coolant from the radiator flows through the engine, absorbs engine heat, and flows back through the radiator's tubes and fins. There, breezed by the incoming airstream, aided by the fan, the radiator transfers to the air some of the heat it has collected. Cooled, the coolant is pumped back through the engine to collect more heat. What does the pumping is the *water pump*.

Involved is a classic case of heat transfer.

Put your hand in front of the radiator after a drive, and the air's warm to hot. It got that way, of course, when the engine, via the radiator, transferred some of its heat to the air, cooling the engine.

En route through the engine's closed heat-transfer loop, some hot coolant may also be diverted, at the driver's command, through the car's heater and defrosters. Their hoses—and in the case of the heater, also its *miniradiator*—are like the hoses of the radiator itself: possible leakers.

All this sounds pretty simple. Basically, it is. What complicates things is the simplest of radiator accessories and one too often taken for granted by car-keepers: the *radiator cap.*

In earlier years the cap was just that—a cap, like a bottle cap, meant to cap the radiator, preventing its water or coolant from sloshing out.

Today the radiator cap, while still preventing splash, is no longer just a radiator cap. It is also a pressure cap. Its function is to allow pressure within the radiator to increase dramatically, which—up to a point—prevents the coolant from boiling at the usual boiling point of water.

Engines work more efficiently when they are hotter—again, up to a point. Also, with

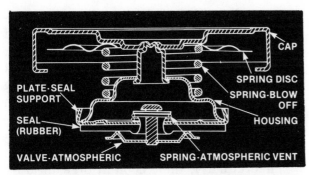

PLATE-SEAL SUPPORT
SEAL (RUBBER)
VALVE-ATMOSPHERIC
CAP
SPRING DISC
SPRING-BLOW OFF
HOUSING
SPRING-ATMOSPHERIC VENT

Radiator's presure cap has changed everything about a kept car's coolant system. Cap isn't the simple thing you think it is or take for granted. (Drawing courtesy of McQuay-Norris, Inc.)

the radiator pressure-capped, you can drive longer, in hotter weather, and to greater altitudes without the radiator boiling, as in earlier days many radiators did.

But the pressure bottled up within your car's radiator, now far greater than earlier, requires some rethinking of the whole radiator-keeping regimen. Keeping your car longer may depend on it.

First, the entire coolant system—including the radiator and its hoses—is under greater pressure and far greater mechanical strain.

Second, when the radiator only seems hot—it's not boiling—its *temperature* may in fact, be far *above* the normal boiling point. Attempt to remove the radiator cap when the engine and radiator are hot, and you risk scalding. Removing the cap, even loosening it, removes the pressure—and *then* the coolant does boil—often instantly. Scalding radiator water fountains up. If, somehow, you avoid a wetting, or worse, the engine can't. Hot water spilling over a hot engine can crack the engine's head or block.

The kind of pressure nowadays inside a radiator causes radiators to leak as in unpressured radiators they seldom did. A leak today is really a pressure leak, and it is harder to plug and stop than a leak with little or no pressure behind it.

One stopgap cure for pressure leaks is to reduce the radiator's internal pressure.

When a kept car's radiator is weakening—springing little leaks here and there—and if you don't want to have a new radia-

tor installed or a major repair job done, at least not right away, you can, instead, reduce its internal pressure. Reducing the pressure will very often stop those little leaks.

How to do it? Simply by replacing your radiator's high-pressure cap with one with a lower pressure rating. Pressure within the radiator will be reduced. Leaks sprung when the radiator was capped at high pressure may subside altogether. And while the engine may not operate at its engineered peak efficiency (running, as it may be, a bit cooler now), it'll generally operate well enough.

Switching to a lower-pressure radiator cap may make it possible to plug those little leaks through a treatment with radiator gunk—the so-called leak stoppers that didn't work as advertised when the radiator was under very high pressure. Putting anything but water and coolant in a radiator, however, risks plugging some of its internal passages.

The risk is no big thing, providing you don't overdose the radiator. If the gunk stops the leaks, you have put off repair or replacement for awhile. If the gunk doesn't stop them, then you have no choice but to drive in for a radiator rework. If the gunk stops them but through an overdose plugs enough of the radiator's innards to cause overheating, you've gambled the small cost of the gunk against the larger cost of radiator rework. And you have lost. Likely you couldn't have gone much longer anyway without professional radiator attention. When the radiator is removed and repaired, the gunk is acid-washed away. In some cases, the gunk treatment is worth a try.

Since higher internal pressure is at the root of what most often ails radiators today, let's see how that pressure is created. What creates it, of course, is the radiator's pressure cap.

But to understand the implication of that pressure, first let's review some highway physics ABCs. At sea level, as you likely learned in school, atmospheric pressure (what at sea level a barometer normally reads) is about 14½ pounds per square

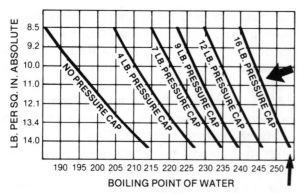

Radiator's pressure cap changes everything—and, if cap bottles within radiator too much pressure, can cause leaks in radiator places that seldom leaked in earlier automotive days, before pressured radiators. Common 16-pound cap raises boiling point of radiator's coolant to more than 250° F. Substituting a slightly lower-rated pressure cap—as text explains— can stop many radiator leaks, yet also give engine the heat it needs to operate near peak efficiency. (Graph courtesy of McQuay-Norris, Inc.)

inch. At sea level and at this usual atmospheric pressure, water—whether on your kitchen stove or in your car's radiator— boils at 212° F.

But put your radiator's coolant under greater than normal sea level pressure, and you effectively *raise* its boiling point. Under pressure, neither water nor radiator coolant boils at the usual 212° F. but at some *higher* temperature. How much higher depends on how much pressure is exerted upon the coolant. The greater the pressure, the higher its temperature can rise before it actually boils.

Radiator pressure caps are available with various pressure ratings. A cap's pressure rating is usually inscribed somewhere on the cap. Some are "4-pound" pressure caps, meaning they are designed to put the radiator under 4 pounds *more* pressure than normal at sea level. Cap pressure ratings go up to 17 pounds or so. Most auto supply stores stock pressure caps with ratings, among others, of 7 pounds, 9 pounds, 12 pounds, and 16 pounds. This latter—the 16-pound pressure cap—is commonly found on car radiators these days. It means that the cap holds the radiator's coolant at 16 pounds per square inch *greater* pressure than normal at sea level.

How does this directly affect the coolant's boiling point? For every one pound of additional pressure put on a car's coolant, the coolant's boiling point is raised about 3¼° F. So a 16-pound pressure cap, putting an additional 16 pounds of pressure on radiator coolant, *raises* the coolant's boiling point 52° F. (16 pounds x 3¼° F. = 52° F.)!

Theoretically, then, coolant pressured by a 16-pound cap can be a sizzling (and scalding) 264° F.—212° F. + 52° F.—before it begins to boil. In practice, not many radiators achieve this kind of superheating before they boil. Still, capped with a 16-pound cap, they can get extremely hot— about 254° F.—before boiling.

Caps with lower ratings hold coolant at lower pressure, reducing the boiling point.

A radiator fitted with a four-pound cap has a boiling point of about 227° F.; with a seven-pound cap, 234° F.; with a nine-pound cap, 239° F., and a 12-pound cap, about 246° F.

If radiator system little leaks develop, replacing the 16-pound cap with a seven-pound cap reduces internal radiator pressure by a sizable nine-pounds while reducing the boiling point by a fairly modest 20° F.

That may be pressure reduction enough to stop most of the bothersome small leaks. Even so, internal radiator pressure and temperature are considerable. That they are explains why radiator hoses frequently spring leaks and why you've got to have your radiator's hoses inspected, visually and physically, now and then.

Radiator hose inspection is one of the few do-it-yourself car chores many carkeepers, even though not car tinkerers, nor with any wish to be, find themselves doing routinely. No tools are involved.

The top radiator hose (of the radiator's usual two major hoses) is, happily, the easiest to see and feel-test (happily, since it's the hose that usually needs replacement more frequently than its bottom-engine partner). The reason the top radiator hose does is that, generally, it's the return hose, meaning it returns hot coolant directly from the hot engine. So it is subject to the highest coolant temperatures of the two. The radiator's bottom hose is the supply hose—it supplies radiator-cooled coolant to the engine. So it, generally, handles cooler water.

Inspecting Coolant System Hoses

With the engine cold: Give each hose, assuming you can reach both, a physical feel-test: squeeze each along its entire length. Any mushiness or sogginess or, by contrast, hardness or brittleness, suggests early replacement. So, of course, do obvious cracks or worn places.

With the engine hot: Visually inspect the hoses for swelling—a sure sign of pressure weakness.

But suppose, with radiator leaks persisting, you drive in to a mechanic or, far better, to a radiator specialist. What can you expect?

You can expect the radiator man to give both the radiator and its cap a *pressure test.* In the first, he wants to see if the cap is maintaining its rated pressure—or, maybe, too much pressure, a major cause of leaks. Second, he pressurizes the radiator itself, often overpressuring it briefly to coax leaking. For both tests he uses a hand air pump that looks like the kind used to inflate bicycle tires, only sturdier. For the radiator "pump-up," he substitutes a special test cap for yours.

Right away, you can often spot the leaks.

The question: Can the radiator be repaired or must it be replaced with new at considerably higher cost?

Certainly most radiators, no matter how bad the leak looks to *you,* can be repaired. And often they can be fixed again and again.

As with many shop-out jobs in car-keeping, whether to repair or to replace often depends more on the condition (fiscal and psychological) of the repairman than on the condition of what's ailing a car. Find a good radiator specialist who, along with you, makes it a little game to fix rather than replace things, and you've found car-

keeping's rarest commodity: a supermechanic.

Long ago I found a super radiator specialist. For more than a decade now, he has medicated my kept car's radiator, but has never yet found it necessary to replace it with a new one. Partly in jest, he has scribbled across the last three bills (sums ranging from $20–$45), "Next time . . . a *new one!*"

That time is yet to come—now nearly 200,000 miles and 13 model years since the radiator was installed, factory-fresh. Meantime, as many car-keepers, I find our keeping-the-radiator game a challenging sport. Not as exciting, granted, as an NFL game on the boob tube, but at least a participation, rather than a spectator, sport.

No doubt about it, the contest—man versus machine—can become part of the sport of car-keeping.

To repair a radiator, the specialist removes it from the car, disassembles it, puts it in an acid bath, and reams out all of the little tubes through which radiator coolant normally circulates.

If he finds a really bad place—and chances are he will—he may seal off that particular part or length of the *core,* which means that while it won't leak (because it's sealed), neither can coolant ever again circulate through that particular run of tubing. Effectively, his repair reduces the total cooling capacity of the radiator.

Will this mean your radiator will operate hotter and boil sooner than before?

Not necessarily. How much of a radiator's total cooling area can be sacrificed in repairs without changing radiator efficiency depends on the car and on the radiator. Older cars were built with capacity to spare. The loss of a few runs of tubing, out of their many, seldom nudges the dashboard temperature gauge (older cars had them, while many cars today don't) even a degree higher. But some newer models, especially the small cars, haven't—as we've said—all that much reserve, if any, built into them.

The decision is up to the radiator specialist. If he's honest, his decision will be honest. There are, however, several ways the car-keeper can boost radiator efficiency—even if the car and its radiator are brand new.

One way is to have installed a replacement fan for the one—usually with four blades—that came with the car. The replacement—with six or more blades—creates a stronger, more cooling windstream on the radiator's backside (engine side). It markedly speeds the radiator's transfer of heat.

Or you might have installed one, but preferably two, small electric fans, powered by the car's battery. The fans are usually, though not always, mounted in front of the radiator. As auxiliaries to the radiator's fan, they likewise increase the radiator's efficiency, but with some notable advantages over engine-powered fans, however many their blades.

Being powered from the battery, the auxiliary electric fans operate at constant speed, regardless of engine speed. They keep the engine cooler in hot weather stop-and-go traffic when the engine's own fan is operating at its slowest and thus at minimal cooling efficiency.

The minielectric fans can also increase the efficiency of an ailing, oft-repaired radiator or of a radiator and cooling system overtaxed by add-on accessories—such as air conditioning. If conditioning was added, a car probably did not have factory air conditioning in the first place. Since it did not, it likely was not factory-equipped with an oversized radiator. Both the minielectrics and the more-than-standard bladed engine fans help an undersized radiator do a more efficient cooling job than it would do without them.

Two other common cooling system potential trouble spots are worth knowing about. One is the *thermostat*, which operates somewhat like a home thermostat. The other is the *water pump*, which operates, well, like a water pump.

In time, the thermostat may fail to operate, meaning that it fails automatically to open and close when coolant temperature signals it to do so.

Thermostat replacement is one of those quick, easy repair jobs. And the thermostat itself is a low-cost item. To replace a thermostat, the mechanic removes two bolts on a front-engine plate that covers the *thermostat well* and its thermostat. He removes the old thermostat, installs a new gasket, pops a new thermostat into its well, and bolts things together again.

The thermostat's function is to warm the engine up quickly when it's started—first thing in the morning, for instance. To do it, the thermostat senses the temperature of the coolant and, finding it chilly, closes, preventing most of the coolant from reaching the radiator. Instead, coolant is routed—uncooled—back to the engine, where it quickly grows hot. Heating up fast, the ever-hotter coolant helps uniformly to warm the cylinders, aiding cold-engine combustion. As coolant temperature rises to the engine's normal operating temperature—in most cars, about 195° F.—the thermostat opens and in effect signals the radiator to take over. With thermostat open, coolant circulates once again through the radiator.

Another coolant system trouble spot is the water pump. It's usually driven by one of the usual three belts on the front of the engine.

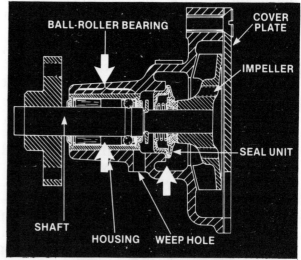

TYPICAL WATER PUMP CUTAWAY
When a water pump goes it is usually because its seals wear, permitting water to reach the bearings. (Drawing courtesy of McQuay-Norris, Inc.)

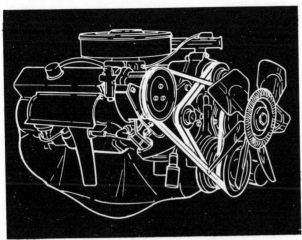

**A TYPICAL MODERN ENGINE'S USE
OF V-BELT DRIVES**

*Front-engine belts, as these three found on most cars,
are the ones that may squeak—but lubricating them
hushes them for a while, at least. The belts drive
various components, including the radiator fan, generator or alternator, power-steering unit, air conditioner's compressor, and sometimes the water pump.
When engine components are not driven by belts, they
are driven by gears powered, like the belts, by the
engine. (Drawing courtesy of McQuay-Norris, Inc.)*

When a water pump goes, you know it.
Sometimes you can hear the grinding of
waterlogged water pump bearings. *Always*
you can see water coming out of the front
of the engine. If it's a lot of water—not
unusual—all dates are off except for the
one you have with a mechanic.

What usually happens is that the pump's
seals, meant to prevent coolant from ever
reaching the pump's bearings, break down
with time and exposure to the engine's
heat. Water reaches the lubricated pump
bearings. And that's that. The cure is a
replacement—usually with an "exchange"
(rebuilt)—water pump.

But, while the usual three drive belts on
the front of the engine, including the one
powering the water pump, don't leak, they
sometimes squeak, screech, and squeal. Periodically, they need attention to hush the
squeal, and replacement as they age and
slacken.

Besides the belt driving the water pump,
there's another that drives the alternator or
generator, which charges the battery. The
third usually drives the power steering.

These, or other drive belts—called V-Belts
because they are V-shaped rather than being flat or round—may also power the air
conditioner's compressor or, occasionally,
an emission control pump.

Drive-belt squeal and screech can usually be hushed—for awhile, at least—with
a few squirts of spray-on lubricant, such as
WD-40, a brand favored by some mechanics. Desqueaking belts is easy. Just be careful, in the process, to keep your hands out
of the moving parts—the fan and the belts
themselves. Thirty seconds, or less, gets
the job done. With the engine running—
thus the belts turning—simply spray some
lubricant on them.

On the other hand, belt squeal and screech
may be a cry for help. The belts may be
trying to tell you something: that, through
wear, they have grown loose and flabby.
And now they are slipping—they're no
longer tight in the V-shaped notches in the
pulleys they are powering. Slipping, they
are overheating. That's because slippage
causes friction and friction causes heat.

Quite aside from the fact that a belt slipping on its pulley isn't delivering the power
it should be delivering to whatever it is
supposed to be powering, there is a fact
that ought to be obvious: overheated by
friction, the belt may have become cracked
and brittle. It could snap—leaving you
without a functioning water pump, power
steering, or a battery charger (generator or
alternator).

But when the mechanic either tightens a
loose belt or replaces it, make sure—in fact,
absolutely insist (which may, admittedly,
require some nerve)—that he uses a little
mechanical *tension gauge* to make sure he
didn't tighten the belt too much. Most mechanics, if they don't use a tension gauge,
simply give a belt a little tug and pro-
nounce it just right. That's *not* good
enough, not with today's lighter-weight,
less husky engines.

If a mechanic overtightens a belt, it can,
in time, do major—and costly—damage to
the engine's front-end gearing, which powers the pulleys on which the belts turn. But
too-tight belting can do even worse: crack

the engine's backbone, its crankshaft. Or it can exert so much pressure on the crankshaft that its bearings—the engine's *main bearings*—go out. That means a major engine overhaul.

If a mechanic won't use a tension gauge, doesn't have one, or has never heard of one, take your car to a mechanic who has and does.

Finally, the matter of radiator coolant. Some things about coolant you already know: that coolant is really a properly proportioned mixture of water and *ethylene glycol*, a kind of alcohol, which used to be called antifreeze but now is called *coolant,* which makes things a bit confusing.

In its proper proportion in your radiator—usually a *50 percent water/50 percent ethylene glycol mix*—coolant does more than merely protect the cooling system and engine against freezing in frigid weather. It is also a corrosion inhibitor, preventing the radiator and the engine's innards from rusting. And, in summer, because the mix has a higher boiling point than water alone, it also helps prevent a radiator from boiling.

Can you, if you drive and live where it seldom freezes or gets all that hot, simply keep the radiator filled with water?

You can, but *not* if you want to stretch out car life and the miles between cooling system repairs.

Many car-keepers, however, think they have coolant enough in their car's cooling systems when they don't. Partly to blame are the coolant makers who claim longer life for coolant than it usually has. Partly to blame is normal radiator "topping off"— when, with the radiator's level down a bit, you (or a station attendant) add some water.

For whatever reasons, pretty soon— sooner than you may think—you no longer have a half-and-half mix of ethylene glycol and water in the radiator. Rather, you likely have a far lower, far less protective proportion of glycol.

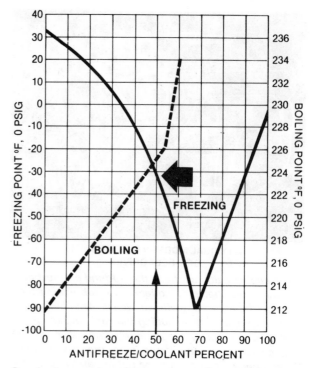

Graph shows why a 50 percent antifreeze/50 percent water coolant mix probably works best in most climates: protects against freezing to -32° F and raises coolant's boiling point to 223° F. (Graph courtesy of McQuay-Norris, Inc.)

How can you be sure? Simply by giving the coolant the *hydrometer test.* The hydrometer—really a little syringe—is available at any auto supply store. You merely immerse—or ask a station attendant to do so—the syringe's plastic tube in the radiator, squeeze the syringe's bulb to draw a sample of coolant, and watch what happens to five or six little colored balls in the top of the tube. The number that float indicates the percentage of glycol to water and thus how much glycol should be added.

Once every 24,000 miles—roughly every two years—the radiator should be drained, flushed (with fresh water run through it under pressure), and refilled with a fresh coolant mix.

Stopping leaks and squeaks? The doing is easy, once you know where they're most likely to crop up and how to stop them if they do.

YEARS-LONGER STRATEGY: RADIATOR

1. Always keep the radiator filled with an ethylene glycol (50 percent)/water (50 percent) coolant mix, unless subzero winter temperatures indicate a higher antifreeze percentage.
2. Never use only water; always a coolant mix.
3. Have the radiator drained, flushed, and filled with fresh coolant mix *at least* every 24 months/24,000 miles
4. Every six months or so, sooner if through overflow, leaking, or boilover the radiator has lost coolant, have the service station attendant hydrometer-test it to see if the 50 percent glycol/50 percent water proportion is maintained.

Hydrometer test of radiator's coolant draws coolant sample in syringe. Floating balls in syringe tube tell percentage of antifreeze in coolant mix.

SYMPTOMS/CAUSES: ENGINE OVERHEATS (Radiator Steams, Boils)

Symptom

Radiator overheats, steams, or boils

Possible Cause

1. Radiator coolant level too low
2. Leak in coolant system or its hoses
3. Fan belt loose
4. Radiator problem: tubes blocked
5. Radiator cap defective; not maintaining system pressure
6. Radiator obstructed (bugs, debris)
7. Thermostat defective

(in winter)
Radiator overheats, steams, or boils

1. Coolant's antifreeze proportion wrong; coolant system freezing
2. All of the above under usual weather conditions

(in summer—hot-weather driving)
Radiator overheats, steams, or boils

1. Coolant's proportion wrong; is not preventing boiling
2. All of the above under usual weather and driving conditions.

Chapter 12: Air Conditioning and Heating
Reinvigorating Comfort Accessories

What the dealer seldom tells you is that your new car has not just one, but two (and possibly three), radiators.

The obvious radiator is the one you keep coolant in. The less obvious is the one, perhaps four to five years and 50,000 miles down the road, that drip-signals its presence. "Something's dripping on my foot!" your passenger exclaims. What's dripping, either because it or its hoses or fittings are leaking, is the *heater's* radiator, hidden under the dash.

While cars with air-cooled engines don't have the problem because they don't car-heat with water, the problem is real enough for the majority of cars because the majority are heated by the same hot coolant that circulates through the engine and *its* radiator.

As a kept car ages, one of the first things to vex its owner is that leaky heater radiator. And, unless it has had regular servicing, the air conditioning system might also be a problem. It simply is no longer cooling as it once did. Or, perhaps, it's no longer cooling at all.

Unless you play it cool and avoid getting hot under the collar—you'll pardon the puns—you seem destined shortly to give an auto heater specialist *and* an auto air conditioning specialist (the one seldom spe-

cializes in both heating *and* air conditioning) some business.

Often you need not—at least, not for a good long while. Consider first that leaky heater radiator. It's a particular bug because it's leaking inside the car, wetting the carpet and your passenger's feet (usually, though not always, the heater's radiator is located under the dash on the passenger side).

Radiator repair or replacement, whether of the engine's or the heater's, can run into money. It is an expense most car-keepers would prefer to avoid.

There are several things you can have done (or perhaps do yourself) to stop the leak and put off repair or installation of a new heater radiator. Before making the decision, and well before your car's heater radiator or its hoses or fittings begin leaking, it's worth knowing how they work.

The basic setup is simple. Some of the hot *coolant* circulating within the engine is routed, by way of a *heater inlet hose,* to the heater's *coils* (the radiator). The hot coolant flows through the radiator and returns to the engine's own radiator, for cooling, by means of the *heater return line.* En route or before, some of the heater's "hot water" (which, of course, is really hot coolant) may also serve the defrosters. No matter;

behind the heater's radiator is an electric fan. Switch on the heater control and the fan blows air through the coolant-hot coils. Result: the heater puts out hot air and everybody is snug and warm.

When the heating and air conditioning are combined in a single air mix unit, as on most cars, things get more complex. Basically, however, the hookup is the same.

What is not the same—and it's critical to any car-keeper's heater decision—is the *heater control valve*. It controls the hot coolant's flow through the heater radiator.

Some control valves are normally always "open," which means that hot coolant always flows through the in-car radiator, though you can't sense it because the fan isn't blowing.

Some control valves are normally always "closed." They permit coolant to flow through the heater radiator only when the heater is on.

Obviously, if yours is a heater whose in-car radiator forever flows with coolant, just turning the heater off won't stop the drip.

So, you must make a decision. Assuming it's still mild weather, or that you can get along without a heater for a while, and assuming coolant flows through the radiator only when you turn on the heater, you can simply turn off the heater and stop the leak. But, if coolant forever flows through the radiator, you—or a mechanic—will have to do more: *bypass* (reroute) the heater's *inlet hose* so that coolant no longer flows through the heater's radiator. The rerouting is a simple thing.

Doing either—bypassing the heater's hot coolant or simply shutting off the heater—accomplishes only one thing: the radiator no longer leaks. But you no longer, either, have heat.

You can, however, have it at virtually no cost if you're willing to try one of those "can't lose" car-keeping experiments. If it works, you may have stopped that heater leak for years. If it doesn't, you are no worse off. Eventually, you'll have to have the heater radiator repaired or replaced professionally.

Here's how the experiment works. As you now know, if before you didn't, the coolant (or at least some of it) that circulates through the car's regular radiator also circulates through the heater's radiator. Thus, any leak-stop quick-fix remedies that seek out small leaks in the regular radiator will also circulate through the heater radiator and likewise seek out leaks there.

There are a number of good leak-stop compounds, most of them powdered copper or aluminum (the latter for aluminum radiators). With the engine running, and in this case the heating also going, you—or a service station man—slowly, as directed on its label, pour the contents of the leak-stop package into the car's up-front radiator. The leak-stop powder or liquid circulates through that radiator and eventually also reaches the heater radiator. And, with a bit of luck, it stops the leaks in it, too.

Among the several inexpensive leak-stop metallic powders or liquids available at most auto supply stores are Aluma, a powder; Weldit, also a powder; Mechanics Leak Stop, a liquid; and Prestone Sealer & Stop Leak, a liquid.

Very often, unless the leak is in the coolant hoses, in the control valve, or in one of the larger-area places of the radiator, little leaks in the heater radiator will be stopped. Sometimes, they can be stopped for years, putting off an otherwise expensive repair. Should leaking again develop, try the leak-stop method again. A time may at last arrive when such quickie methods no longer work. Time enough, then, to face up to a heater radiator repair or replacement.

Your car's air-conditioning system is another matter. It is far more complex. When it fails to operate or to operate well enough to keep a chill on things, you usually need an auto air-conditioning specialist.

That you may is too often the fault of a single act of neglect by car-keepers: failure, *every* month, in winter as well as summer, to run the air conditioning at least five to 10 minutes.

Doing so, the system's key (and most expensive component), its *compressor*, self-lubricates its own moving parts, especially its refrigerant seals. Left unlubed, the seals grow brittle and shrink. And the system's vital and volatile *refrigerant* escapes, leaving you without air conditioning. In time, you will also have a sizable bill for compressor overhaul.

Recommended for nearly all air-conditioning systems is a once-a-year spring checkup, which includes recharging the system with its vital refrigerant, a compressed liquid fluorocarbon called R-12, the *R* for refrigerant.

Let's see how the air conditioning works and why its R-12 refrigerant is its veritable lifeblood.

Car air conditioning, like any air conditioning, works by manipulating the refrigerant circulating through its components, now changing it from a liquid to a gas and back again—now increasing its pressure and temperature, now reducing them both. To do it, and quite literally to absorb heat from inside the car and carry it outside (the reason a car's air-conditioned interior *feels* cold), it needs three basic and major components.

The under-dash radiator-like *evaporator* absorbs in-car heat in order to maintain the gaseous refrigerant within its coils as a gas. It passes this now car-heat-laden refrigerant gas to the *compressor*, which is located under the hood and is belt-driven by the engine. The compressor, both a refrigerant pump and what its name implies, compresses the evaporator's heat-laden gaseous refrigerant into a high-pressure gas. Then it passes it on to the *condenser*, installed in front of the car's radiator. As the heat-laden refrigerant gas passes through the radiator-like condenser, the airstream cools the gas, thus transferring its heat load to the air, and the cooled refrigerant changes back to a liquid. That liquid is pumped back to the evaporator where, changing once more to a gas, it picks up another load of in-car heat. And you and your passengers ride contented— because the air conditioning is working.

The problem is, it doesn't always work.

Although obviously a lot can go wrong with the air-conditioning system other than

CHECK OUT CONDITION OF COOLANT CHARGE

Be sure to read all instructions carefully before proceeding. If you are inexperienced in the use of this product, obtain professional help before using. Use of goggles or safety glasses is recommended.

Check sight glass, located on top of filter drier, storage tank or fender well, after operating system for 10 minutes at maximum cooling.

Left: (Fig. A) Slow-moving bubbles in sight glass indicate system is in need of a slight charge

Left: (Fig. B) Heavy or large bubbles indicate system is very low on charge and may require more than 1 can

Left: (Fig. C) Oil streaks on sight glass indicate complete absence of Refrigerant 12 and entire system must be recharged.* Use no more than 3 cans

*Note: As a double-check to determine if system is without charge, run engine at fast idle . . . turning magnetic clutch on and off . . . bubbles should then be seen or entire system must be recharged.

Telltale refrigerant flow patterns in air-conditioning system's sight glass *reveal if more refrigerant is needed. (Drawing courtesy of COLD SHOT/Radiator Specialty Company.)*

simply losing some of its refrigerant and needing more, putting more in—or having it put in—if it needs it may prevent a never-cheap visit to the air-conditioning specialist.

What tells you or a service station man if the system does, indeed, need more refrigerant, is its little *sight glass*. Through it— once you have located it under the hood— you can observe the flow of refrigerant in the system to see whether or not refrigerant is needed and, if so, approximately how much.

For the sight glass to read accurately, the air conditioning must be run for at least 10 minutes at its maximum chill setting. Then, the conditioner still at maximum chill, through the sight glass any of several tell-tale refrigerant flow patterns will begin to emerge, each with a distinctive meaning:

- *Clear* (without bubbles or oil streaks): *Usually means fully charged, no refrigerant needed.*
- *Slow-Moving Bubbles: Usually means slightly low, could use slight booster charge of refrigerant.*
- *Many Heavy and Large Bubbles,* which seem to be boiling: *Usually means system is very low, needs at least one 14-ounce can of refrigerant, possibly two cans.*
- *Oil Streaks—No Bubbles: Usually*

means system has no refrigerant, needs complete recharge. But do not use more than three 14-ounce cans.

The recharging procedure is a bit tricky. Better have the station man do it. Recharge kits with one 14-ounce can of refrigerant cost $7.50–$10 at most auto supply stores; additional cans, $1.50–$2.50.

If recharging, as the sight glass indicated, doesn't put a renewed chill on things—its duration at least summer-long—then, as any car-keeper, you'll have to concede that, while it was a cool and logical try, it didn't work.

Your next stop? At the air-conditioning specialist's shop.

YEARS-LONGER STRATEGY: AIR CONDITIONING

1. Avoid turning on air conditioning at high engine or highway speeds.
2. Operate air-conditioner *at least* five to 10 minutes *at least* once (twice is better) a month, *year-round.*
3. Have system's compressor belt drive checked for wear and tension when you have other engine belting checked.
4. Wash the conditioner's radiator-condenser—mounted in front of car's radiator—when you wash the car.
5. Annually (best in Spring), have air-conditioning system checked, serviced, and, if needed, recharged with refrigerant.
6. If you skip or delay annual servicing, don't skip check of air-conditioning compressor's oil level.

Chapter 13: Bodywork
New Look for Old

If you let your body go to pot, it is slow to get back into shape. The same thing happens to your car's, only sometimes it never really ever gets back into shape.

Bodywork—what to have done, where to have it done, and when to do it—is strategically among the most debatable decisions in car-keeping.

Owners who are most intimately caught up in the economics of keeping a car longer—longer, perhaps, then they have ever kept a car before—seem most sharply divided on that decision of *when*—when to have bodywork done. Automotively speaking, there are two lanes of thought.

The let-them-accumulate keepers do just that: they may let three to five years of fender bangs, door nicks, and body bruises pass by before finally taking their car into a body shop for what amounts to the works: body rework *and* a paint job.

The fix-it-fast keepers have most things fixed as soon as they happen. They dent a fender, and the next day their car is in for repairs. Let just a few nicks riffle a door, and they consign the car for denicking and a touch-up.

Involved in the "when" decision are both economics and psychology.

The fix-it-fasters insist there are sizable advantages to keeping a car up and never permitting its body to go shabby.

First, repair bills may be piddling to modest, with only a few nicks to fill, sand, and touch over. Then, too, the doing gets done in a day or so—occasionally, the very same day. So they seldom have to give up their cars for long. And if the repair is more major—say, somebody rams them in traffic or on a parking lot—they invariably collect from the other driver's insurance company. They may end up paying nothing, or next to it, for the repair.

Moreover, the fix-it-fast practitioners say flatly that were they to let things slide, they would likely trade in rather than fix up their cars, battered and beaten as they might become if body-neglected over the years.

"By then," shrugs a fix-it-fast believer, "I would have lost all pride in ownership . . . and simply no longer want to own or drive it."

For many who believe in fixing it fast, there is deeper psychological motivation. "A car," analyzes another who fixes his now, "tells a lot about its owner. When I see a car pitted with dents, crumpled fenders, and body bangs, I *already* know all I want to know about the person driving *that* car. I wouldn't drive a car that told *that* about me."

But many let-them-accumulate advocates sharply disagree. They contend that it is far less costly to have everything fixed at once, rather than piecemeal. Besides, they say, in an age when one can scarcely drive into a parking lot without driving out dented, the time and trouble, to say nothing of finding other means of transportation while a car is being fixed, become unconscionable.

What about collecting insurance when the other driver is at fault? The accumulators go right ahead and collect if they can. They accumulate the money (at least some of them say they do) in their bank accounts toward what one calls, "the grand fix-it-day"—the day, finally, when they drive in for accumulated body repair.

Analysis of the two body repair strategies shows this:

1. Having repaired now what needs repairing spreads out the cost of bodywork. Barring major collision damage, the car-keeper is seldom hit with a body bill that hurts.
2. Even a half dozen quite modest bodywork bills spread over the years usually add up to more than had the car-keeper saved up his bodywork for a single rejuvenation.
3. Even so, again barring major collision damage, the fix-it-fast owner often avoids what most car-keepers should attempt to avoid: a total repainting. The repaint, if properly done, can total more than all of the body repairs combined. And it seldom duplicates, either in appearance or durability, the original factory paint job. What's more, if a paint job is needed, its considerable cost, added to the considerable cost of the accumulated bodywork, can deliver a one-time bill that evokes mental anguish and monetary paralysis. Sometimes paralyzed, too, is the keeper's resolve to keep the car. And strategy schedule budgeting can be thrown months out of kilter.
4. It is also true, a survey among car-keepers shows, that the more clobbered their car's body becomes, the more diminished their pride in ownership. If there is a single factor that urges many to abandon car-keeping

and to trade in what they drive, it is what one owner calls "my former junkyard on wheels, which got that way because I neglected body repairs."

Somehow a car's visual depreciation looms far larger in the keep-it/dump-it decision than the out-of-sight condition of its innards. Many an owner has abandoned car-keeping not because there was anything particularly wrong with the way the car ran, but because of its diminished image. Such drivers mortgage their paychecks for a new $10,000 model, when $500 worth of bodywork, and perhaps less, would have remade both their own driving esteem and their car's image.

Psychologists believe that prolonged neglect of a car's appearance—particularly its outward appearance by owners who care about appearances—is a kind of reinforcement mechanism. In time, the visual neglect reinforces a decision actually reached long before: to sell and buy new. But until diminished appearance reinforces an owner's earlier decision, he cannot justify, in his own mind, what all along he had intended to do. Bodywork neglect reinforces and finally justifies that decision.

What, then, is involved in bodywork? And where and how can you get your car's body repaired best for least?

Bodywork is metalwork—unless, of course, your car's body is fiberglass, as some now are.

When you take your car into a body shop the estimator gives it a quick walk-around. He knows what you may not: that many of the "dish dents" (the pushed-in places on fenders) can be popped out in less than 10 seconds' time. And he knows that even grislier dents pull out with only a little more doing. To pull out a deep dent, bodymen drill holes from the outside through the dent place, insert a special pulling tool, and simply pull the depressed place back into fender shape.

Dozens of special bodywork tools make quick work of average dents, even of push-ins: when a whole side, rear or fender has

Body shop man knows what you may not know: a pulling tool can pull this dent into fender shape in seconds.

been pushed out of shape. The tools in the body repairman's arsenal (and some treat it as such, doing a slam-bang job) are fascinating.

Dent pullers, their tips inserted through a hole drilled in the dent, do what their name implies—fast. So do *vacuum suction cup pullers*. Like a powerful plumber's plunger, they vacuum-attach themselves to the metal and in a single split-second effort pull out the dent. *Body panel straighteners* include a powerful jack that can exert pressure enough to quickly align hoods, bumpers, and fenders.

Other tools in the bodyman's kit include air-operated *body-smoothing hammers*, *bumping anvils* (to backstop blows from rubber-headed *bumping hammers*), *fender flanges*, and powered *paint strippers*, which literally flail paint from metal due for repainting.

But the Cat-scan of the best-equipped body shop is its *frame straightener*, a muscular hydraulic rack that, like a chiropractic automaton, can manipulate back to rights an auto frame wronged in a shuddering crash.

Given even this bodywork doctor's kit, body panels that have been cut through as though by a can opener may be more economically and quickly fixed by replacement

than by repair. And a car body, like its human counterpart, is an anatomical thing; its every panel and chrome strip are identified by name. Thus, there are *rear quarter panels, inner rear wheel panels, front lower pillar post panels, rocker panels, corner caps,* and *door threshold panels,* to list but a few.

Nonetheless, the real art of body repair lies less in the pulling and straightening of body damage, or even panel replacement,

Through-the-metal rip in this rear-end panel means that it must be replaced.

Once dents have been pulled out, the really skilled work begins: filling and sanding rough places that remain.

than in the artful final cover-up: the application of fillers (special epoxylike filling compounds) that fill in the still rough places. And, finally, there is the *shaping, sanding, priming* (preliminary bonding paint layer), and *painting*—the successive spray application of layers and layers of paint. There is obviously a layered and look difference between a two-pass (two-layer) cheapie paint job and a 20-layer one, which may overcoat the most expensive bodywork jobs. Both, initially and to the untrained eye, may look the same, but not after a relatively few months or years.

Shopping for Bodywork

The same car-owners who regularly shop half a dozen department stores before making a final decision leave their cars for body repairs at the first shop that hands them a job estimate. Nor would any furniture shopper buy without first running hands over the finish. Yet few, if any, bodywork shoppers run hands, much less eyes, over representative samples of in-progress bodywork in a body shop. Neither would a department store shopper agree to a purchase without the salesperson first itemizing all of the costs. Yet, invariably, bodywork shoppers do.

Get three estimates—at least. Assuming, as is often the case, that *you* are paying for the bodywork (it is not insurance work), nonetheless take a bodywork tip from the insurance companies, the single largest buyers of bodywork in the nation. Usually they demand three itemized estimates. This does not mean, however, that they necessarily choose the cheapest. And neither, necessarily, should you.

On the advice of friends who have used them or from the *Yellow Pages,* pick three or four body shops. From each one get an estimate in writing, with *every* item, from chrome trim to rubber molding replacement, listed. Also, ask as any savvy car-keeper asks, to look over some of their handiwork—work in progress.

In the shop, inspect in particular cars that seem ready for painting. They are eas-

ily distinguishable because the paint they are wearing is the initial, or *primer,* coat. Generally, it is a flat, dullish-looking paint, running to grey or off-white. At this stage, just before final painting, you can tell a lot about the work underneath.

Quick-judging a body shop's work. Walk to the front or rear of a car that is being repaired. Squint down the sides and fenders. Do you see, beneath the grey primer coat, any ripples, rough places, or bulges? Fingertip appraisal will likely confirm your visual judgment. In appraising finish coat makeready, however, the eyes are more discerning than the hands. Unless what's under that primer coat is all but perfect, hand the shopman his estimate and cross *that* place off your list. No amount of overpainting will correct shoddy undercoat work. It will show, no matter how layered the final finish.

Keeping body shops honest. If the estimate the shopman hands you indicates that he plans to install replacement panels, parts, molding, or trim, jot down two things for your own reference: the *precise* description of each item ("inner rear wheel panel") and its *part number,* if listed, and the shop's cost estimate for each. Estimators have a practiced way of scrawling replacement prices, part descriptions, and part numbers that make them difficult to read—sometimes on purpose. Having jotted them down, tell the estimator that you are considering furnishing most of the job's add-ons yourself, for him to install.

At this point, he is apt either to agree (indicating that his add-on pricing is probably fair) or tell you his shop doesn't operate that way (an almost sure sign that he has doubled and tripled the cost to you of virtually every add-on). If he agrees that you may supply most or some of the add-on parts, ask him to refigure his estimate to *exclude* what you plan to furnish.

Now, you have *two* estimates: one, the bodywork job, its every part supplied by the body shop; the other, the same job, *minus* the parts you expect to buy from a junk parts place or from a dealer.

So calculated a ruse—for it may only be

that, should you later decide not to supply the parts—accomplishes two things. For one, it often establishes on the spot the shop's parts pricing honesty. If parts costs are overinflated, thus proportionally a large part of the total estimate, few bodywork shops will permit you to supply your own parts. For another, you've acquired a shopping list. Buying the parts yourself for major collision bodywork may save you several hundred dollars and sometimes much more.

Dealing in the dealer. With your itemized parts list in hand, stop by the parts department of the new car dealer who sells your make of car. Show the parts man your list and ask the price *he* charges for the most important items. If there is a significant difference—the dealer asks $100 for a replacement part listed at $150–$200 by the body shop—you have two choices, both of them money savers.

You can order the parts, deliver them (or have them delivered, which some parts departments do) to the body shop, and perhaps see your bodywork bill reduced $200–$400 below what the shop proposed charging when it furnished the replacement parts. Or you can save even more—about 50 percent off the dealer price—shopping for the parts at an auto wrecking yard.

If you haven't recently visited one, and likely you haven't, you're in for a surprise. Today's auto dismantler is no junk yard of yesteryear, even though it may appear so to you. The dismantler is a specialist in salvaging (often from wrecks) and selling good used auto parts—parts no more, and sometimes less, used than your own kept car's.

Shopping the auto dismantlers has a number of advantages besides saving you 50 percent, even 60 percent or more on bodywork and other parts. The dismantlers are extremely knowledgeable. They can often find the part you want in a hurry and deliver it now—the same day (new car dealers may take two to three days for hard-to-get parts).

And, because he is a parts expert, dealing in parts from all makes of cars, a dismantler, looking at your bodywork shopping list, can often substitute an exact part, even though its part number may differ from the one the bodywork shop noted down. Exact parts substitution, though the part may come from a different model of car than yours, is possible because Detroit, especially, practices commonization: one part designed to fit many models made by the same manufacturer.

Dismantling experts know which parts are "commonized." A new car dealer's parts man may not.

When it comes to replacement metal, it makes no difference—so long as there are no dents or rust—whether the part is new (purchased from a new car dealer) or used (purchased from an auto wrecking yard). The part is sanded, primed, and painted anyway. And, whether new or used, it looks the same once installed and finished.

What is often vastly different is the price you pay.

Segmenting the work to save. There are other ways to save on bodywork. Among the best of them is to segment the work, having one shop, which does excellent *body repairing* for less than most other shops in town, do what it does best—the basic metalwork. Another, specializing in *painting,* but also reasonably priced, do what it does best: painting.

Finding such specialized shops is not usually all that difficult, especially in larger towns and cities. That they do exist is not only emphasized by the shops themselves, but lies in the very way they came to be. Many were founded by specialists in bodywork *or* body painting, but usually not in both. Grown up, then, are what might be called "UPPER/lower case" shops. Typically, the advertising of one might read "*AUTO PAINTING* and bodywork" or, conversely, "*BODY REPAIR.* We paint, too." The uppercase (capital letter) emphasis plainly proclaims each shop's specialty and just as plainly indicates that the other, painting or metalwork, is more for customer convenience than a shop specialty (or, in fact, a shop skill).

Let's see how it might work for you.

Shop A, a *bodywork specialist,* hands you an itemized estimate showing that, of the total $600 it's asking for the job, $250 is for bodywork and $350 for painting.

Shop B, a *painting specialist,* comes in with the same total in its job estimate, $600, but with some differences. It's asking $250 for the painting and $350 for the bodywork.

Split the work. Let *Shop A,* the bodywork specialist, do what it does best for less—for $250. And have *Shop B,* the painting specialist, do what it does best, likewise for less—$250. In total you'll pay $500—$100 less than the job total asked by each. And you'll get the *best* from each.

Actually, major collision damage estimates may vary by several, even many, hundreds of dollars. It is possible in such a situation not merely to buy what each specializing shop does best, but overall to save $200–$500 and more in the doing.

There are still other ways to save.

Take your car to school. Many local high schools and colleges have auto bodywork classes and courses. While their students are not professionals, they are as often teenage car buffs. If not, they probably would not have enrolled in the class. Many are surprisingly skilled at routine bodywork. Should they not be, the class instructor—usually a bodywork pro—is.

Not all school classes accept outside work. But many do. Virtually none charges for the doing, but only for needed parts and paint.

Taking a car to a bodywork school for repair is little different, really, from sending the kids, on rare occasion, to a barber college. Nothing all that much can go wrong. You hope, of course, for the best. And sometimes you get it.

But even should a place here and there on a class bodywork job be less than you had hoped for, you can always have it righted by a professional shop. And for modest money, since the pro shop won't have to start from scratch.

Often, however, the school shops do a far better job than you might have reason to expect. In a way, their students are as skilled as many apprentices who, in some pro body shops, do the lion's share of the makeready anyway.

Admittedly, shopping for bodywork, like shopping for bodywork parts or shopping for anything else, takes time. Only you can judge whether or not you have it and whether taking it will repay your time and trouble.

For minor ding and dent repairs, savings are apt to be negligible and the trouble not worth it. For major collision damage, or bodywork accumulated over the months and years, the time and trouble—assuming you are paying the bill—may be rewarding and may very well add up to savings few car-keepers can afford to ignore.

RUST: THE KEPT CAR'S NUMBER ONE ENEMY

How, logically, can you plan on keeping a car years longer if, sooner rather than later, it may physically rust away? There are several answers.

First, a car need not rust away if *you apply strict wintertime maintenance,* which means giving it a *thorough* washing, especially the underframe and underparts, *every week.* And, if *it has not already been factory rust-protected,* you can prevent the car from rusting away by spending the $100–$300 for a professional, warranted rust protection job. Such work is done by new car dealers and various franchised specialists who apply such trade named antirust treatments as Ziebart, Tuff-Kote, Rusty Jones, Poly-Gard and others. *You cannot do the job yourself and do it right.*

If your car is not new — and most kept cars are not

— have it inspected for rust, especially for the first signs of rusting. Have a body shop (likely the same one who did the rust inspection) repair what rust damage you have — now. Then have it professionally treated by one of the antirust specialists.

Rusting that is serious enough to threaten car life is generally, with some exceptions (such as in mountain snow areas in the West), confined to the 24 so-called "Salt Belt states" and to the Distict of Columbia. The Salt Belt covers Connecticut, Delaware, Illinois, Indiana, Iowa, Kansas, Kentucky, Maine, Maryland, Massachusetts, Michigan, Minnesota, Missouri, Nebraska, New Hampshire, New Jersey, New York, Ohio, Pennsylvania, Rhode Island, Vermont, Virginia, West Virginia, and Wisconsin. These states are visited by heavy winter snow. To combat it, and to keep roads open, state authorities use salt on streets, roads, and highways.

Although the average car's cheap steel ("cheap" by steel industry grading, even in some $25,000 cars) will gradually rust wherever moisture collects, salt vastly speeds corrosion in the Salt Belt. There, a car body, not rust-protected, can become rust-pitted — even rust through in places — over a winter's time.

In the last several years, however, U.S. car makers, in particular, have factory rust-protected their products. Now rust-prone body panels are routinely galvanized and zinc coated, the entire body dipped in antirust primer, and afterward further corrosion treated.

All General Motors new cars get its Fisher Body Division's antirust treatment. GM's 1981-introduced "J" cars (Chevrolet, Pontiac, and Cadillac) likewise receive the full antirust works. Besides an eight-stage phosphate metal cleaning for starters, the entire body is submerged in a rust-resistant primer. Particularly rust-prone body parts — hoods, fenders, doors, trunk lids, and others — are fabricated from special metals, including zinc-coated steel, with a zinc primer. And the new "J" car body is designed to minimize the entrapment of water, dirt, and especially road salt, the culprits in body rusting.

So convinced are auto makers that the corrosion-proofing works that nearly all now warrant their new cars against rusting. General Motors covers all of its cars with a 36-month unlimited-mileage no-rust warranty. American Motors does even better. Beginning with its 1980 modles, it has guaranteed against body corrosion for fully five years.

Older Salt Belt cars, however, not now rust-proofed, will rust. The only way to prevent it is to know how rusting happens, where it is likeliest to happen, and how to combat it.

The "how" is easily explained. You drive through salted ice, snow, and slush. The stuff works into your car's unseen, hard-to-reach "box" areas — the inner welded sections of body and frame. In time the snow and slush melt and disappear. Left behind is a residue of salt.

Salt is highly corrosive to iron, the main constitu-

ent of an automobile's low-grade steel. Salt causes the steel (mainly the iron in it) to oxidize, or rust. The salt deposit, layered over inner welds, hidden body structures, the underside of fenders, and inside the lower body, lies there waiting to be reactivated. What reactivates it is moisture. Any moisture, even humidity, causes the residual salt to resume its deadly oxidation of the cheap steel to which it clings (stainless steel is not affected by road salt).

One day you notice a rust spot on a fender or body panel (it need not be a lower body panel, because salt works its way upward, carried by wet and moisture, into the doors themselves).

New studies — including research at Cornell University — show, oddly, that rust action on cars, mostly road salt triggered, is actually *20 to 30 times greater in spring* than in winter (when most of the salt was laid). The reason is rising temperatures, which, like humidity, trigger salt-caused oxidation. Cornell researchers warn Salt Belters *not* to leave their cars in heated garages in winter. Heat increases salt corrosion.

The durability of a car's steel to salt, say these same researchers, depends on the amount and timing of winter (and early spring) washings and maintenance.

If you drive in the Salt Belt, your car, even if rust-protected, must be washed at least every week during salt-use periods. What counts most is washing the underside — especially under fender wells and other enclosed areas, such as doors. Paint doesn't rust; the metal beneath and behind it does.

If you use a commercial car wash, ask if the water they use is fresh (used once) or recycled (used over and over again). Recycled water, finds the Cornell team, often contains significant amounts of road salt. Do not patronize a car wash that recycles its wash water. You are merely compounding the rusting.

Although weekly car washes in winter are all but mandatory for Salt Belt car-keepers, even pressure washing or steam cleaning (which is better) beneath the car will not and cannot reach the boxed-in structures most prone to rusting.

What will reach those areas is a professional antirust protection treatment. And, again, this is all but mandatory for car-keepers in the Salt Belt unless their cars are already factory treated. If you're in doubt as to whether your car — a late 1970s, early 1980s model — was factory protected, check with your dealer.

During the some three-hour professional process, using three to six gallons of a spray-on but quick-hardening protectant (usually a petroleum-metallic mixture), every hidden under-car and in-car area is coated. To do this, applicators must drill into "box" areas, remove interior door panels, loosen trim, and generally dismantle whatever blocks spray access to rust-prone places. The car is hoisted and worked on from underneath as well as from all sides. When the job is finished, the holes are plugged, the panels and trim replaced. And the protectant, first hardening to paraffin consistency, then to a soft, puttylike plastic, air seals the metal — hopefully for all times. Sealed from air, metal cannot oxidize, and thus cannot rust.

The better commercial rust treatment systems, though often working through franchised local dealers who apply the rust-protective material, warrant their work — sometimes for upwards of five years (for new cars), less for older ones.

But read *carefully* their usually *limited* warranties. The Federal Trade Commission, alerted by car owner complaints that some antirust treatment operators do not abide by their warranties, is presently investigating the rust proofers.

Most domestic auto makers, as we've noted, now rust protect their products. And more: they warrant them against rusting during the car's first three to five years.

Typically, since 1980, American Motors (AMC) has delivered its cars with Ziebart Factory Rust Protection at no added cost. AMC warrants the protection for five years, with no mileage limitation. During this time, AMC will pay for the repair or replacement of any part it supplied, except exhaust system components, which under normal use develop "perforation from corrosion."

But AMC's warranty, as others, requires that you adhere to some commonsense rust-preventive rules to protect your car and its antirust treatment. Among AMC's warranty provisions: collision-damaged panels may be replaced *only* by new factory-approved or authorized panels. Approved panels and other collision-replacement parts must, themselves, be rust-proofed within two months following installation. If not, they fall out of (are no longer covered by) AMC's antirust warranty.

Where design or other factory methods fail to insure against rusting, massive parts replacement or repair reimbursements have recently been ordered by the Federal Trade Commission (FTC). In 1981, for one example, American Honda Motor Co. signed an FTC consent agreement, under which the Japanese car maker agreed to replace or reimburse repairs of rusted-out fenders on those of its 1975–1978 Civics and Accords registered to owners in the Salt Belt states. While certainly not involving them all, the order potentially affected some 700,000 Hondas sold in the salt area during those years.

FTC investigators concluded that Honda's rust problem was "caused by a fender design that allows moisture and road debris, including salt, kicked up by the front tires, to become lodged underneath the fender."

While the FTC did not say so, the implication of its order to Honda bluntly implied what every Salt-Belter must, sooner rather than later, face up to: *Antirust protection, whether factory or commercially applied, is absolutely mandatory if you drive in the Salt Belt.*

Anything less — including store-bought remedies that promise a quick cure — will fail. And while commercial rust protection is not free, it is a small price to pay for protecting for years longer the useful life — and body appearance — of your car.

YEARS-LONGER STRATEGY: RUST PROTECTION

1. If you drive in the 24 Salt Belt states or the District of Columbia, and your car is not already factory antirust treated, have it professionally rust-protected *now.* Waiting even another winter may make it too late.
2. Treated or not, Salt Belt cars must be washed — with emphasis on their salt-prone undersides — at least every week during road salt periods (winter and early spring).
3. In winter, Salt Belters, especially, should not park overnight in a heated garage. Its heat and humidity trigger residual salt's corrosive action.
4. Elsewhere, especially in humid or ocean-breezed areas, inspect at least annually for signs of rusting. Any progressively rusting area should be repaired and repainted.
5. In the Salt Belt, particularly, if you add new parts (a fender, say, to repair collision damage), have the part rust-protected immediately, unless it is a factory-approved (already treated) part.
6. Wherever you find it, just don't let rust go. Untreated, rust will grow progressively worse.

Chapter 14: Paint and Polish
Showroom Glitter from a Can

What surprises a lot of car-keepers is that they actually didn't need that paint job they were so sure they needed. Recalls one among the surprised, "Sure, I'd neglected it to hell. The paint looked awful, with streaks running down the roof and the hood and trunk lid faded and blotched. I'd even made an appointment with a paint shop to bring it in. And then I got the *shine*. . . ."

The "shine" is what often snatches an about-to-be-painted kept car from the spray booth. And if not for all times, certainly for another few years or so. A "shine" is a paint rescue. Like the surgeon's face peel, which doesn't always work, the shine doesn't always work either. But as a car-lift it probably works as often as a face-lift. Both are worth a try for failing good looks.

A "shine" is, in fact, just that: a professional polishing job that, at its best, is considerably more. In the process, the pro literally peels away—more correctly, rubs away—the top layer or layers of paint. To do so he uses various *rubbing compounds* and *cleaners*—mild abrasives formulated to remove the outer, oxidized layer of paint. If he is careful, and if enough paint layers remain so he is always working "in paint" (not breaking through to the primer coat or, far worse, to bare metal), what is often laid bare is a fresh underlying coat of the car's original paint.

Once the peel job is finished, the door nicks and gravel pocks touched up, the rest of the job becomes a routine pro polish: first a glaze, then one or more coats of top-grade wax.

Results are often amazing. Moreover, the "shine" goes a long way toward restoring the paint job to its factory condition. It lets you retain the original paint and put off any thought of a repainting for perhaps years more. And it costs only what the best of pro polishers charge for their work: perhaps $45–$75 for the four to six hours it takes.

Good "shine" pros and their shops (though some work out of car wash places, gas stations, and the like) are not hard to find. It does, however, take some shopping—and a visit to the pro while he's working—to spot a pro who takes the time and has the skill to do the job right. The skill is not in the glazing and polishing. Almost any pro polisher does that well enough. The skill lies in peeling away just enough paint and not too much.

Will it really look like new? That depends. It will almost certainly shine like new. And if, thereafter, you keep up its appearance with regular waxings, you won't be disappointed. But, if the paint is actually down to primer in places, or very thin, if stains and blotches have worked through all the factory original's paint layers, they'll still be there. But with things shining as they will be, they probably will not be overly obvious. Likely you can live with them. For the $250–$500 difference between a "shine" and a new middling paint job, a car-lift isn't all that difficult to live with.

A repainting is another ball game. And if it's not done right, you can easily strike out and find the new paint chipping and peeling only months after it was put on.

There are paint jobs and paint jobs, as well as obvious differences between the one-day, one-coat synthetic enamel $79.50 quickie and a $750–$1500 multilayered lacquer job.

Down to Bare Metal

There is no substitute for taking off all of the paint and getting down to the original metal. It takes doing, which takes time and boosts the cost of the job. One of the things bare-metaling does is eliminate the "alligatoring"—the leather-look, crosshatch lines—common to long-neglected paint. You can paint over them, but inevitably they reappear. Only bare-metaling eliminates them. Stripping to bare metal also gives the car painter the opportunity he needs to start from scratch.

Preparation

Once down to bare metal, the real work—prepping—begins. Whatever needs to be done to prepare the now bare metal for priming—metalwork, filling, reconstruction, and sanding—must be done. For if what's underneath is faulty, everything sprayed over it will be faulty. One reason a good paint job may well keep a car in the shop for a week, even longer, is the time needed to strip and prep it for painting.

Primer Coat

The primer must be compatible with the type of paint—synthetic enamel, enamel, acrylic, or lacquer—that will be sprayed over it.

Preparation of the primer surface, as preparation of the metal beneath it, is critical. Otherwise the job will not look as it should. And worse: finish coats, in time, will lose their adhesion with the primer, and perhaps with one another, and begin to chip, blister, and peel. In quality paint shops, the primer coat, once dry, is hand-sanded with very fine, furniture-finishing-quality wet grit emery paper.

If you know what wet grit paper looks like, and don't see any of it lying around a paint place's floor, you can be pretty sure they skip this step, which is among the more time-consuming. But it is a necessary step in any good paint job.

Finish Coats

Most average-price car paint jobs get a couple of passes with the spray gun—no more. Some get only one. Really superb jobs may get as many as 16 or more. That's right, 16 coats of paint (usually lacquer). And after each, the paint is rubbed out—a skill in itself. Low- to medium-priced jobs aren't rubbed out at all.

Final results often depend on the sprayer's skill. The less than skilled indelibly leave their marks: runs, orange peel (paint pile-up that resembles the peel of an orange), bubbles and overspray. The latter occurs when parts not to be painted—chrome, molding, mirrors, tires, and windows—are poorly masked and get painted anyway.

Bake Dry

Whether a paint job should get, or necessarily profits from, a heat-lamp baking depends on a number of factors, including the type of paint used. Most quickie car paintings, as well as the factory-original itself, are baked. One reason is to production-speed drying. Even so, it is generally conceded that it is the bake treatment that makes the factory original so durable and all but unduplicable outside the factory. Many medium-priced paint jobs, as well as some very expensive ones, are merely air-dried—left standing to dry unaided.

A new paint job should be garaged its first night to avoid dewing. It should not be washed for at least a week, and then it should only be hosed off, if you must, with cold water. Neither should it be put through a regular car wash for a month. New paint may not harden fully for 12–14 days. Some paints take even longer.

Questions and Answers

Here are questions car-keepers frequently ask about paint jobs—and some answers.

Can an average repainting equal the original factory job?

No, virtually nothing less than a very expensive, custom, multilayered repainting equals the original. A repainting, as a rule, lacks the factory original's durability.

Is there any reason, when repainting, not to change the car's color?

There are lots of reasons why you should not, but they all go down the drain if you really hate your car's present color.

As for why not: First, factory colors—by year, make and model—are distinctive (other, say, than black and white). A different color may depreciate both a car's looks and its value. Second, the original color will almost certainly show up—not in the main body paint, but in out-of-the-way places. No sprayer can totally erase all evidence of the original paint. Out of the way or not, they brand a car "repainted." Car appraisers routinely scan door edges and as routinely declare a car "a repaint," which depreciates from its value as a resale. So, unless—and even if—the car is stripped to bare metal, stick with the factory color.

A final reason not to change color: you may never again find the new color available, and certainly not from the car dealer who does stock (or can get) factory colors. Touching up or repainting, say, a new door installed after a collision, can become a color-match impossibility.

Is it really worth bothering to inspect a paint shop's in-progress work as some indication of its work quality?

Absolutely. (See Chapter 13, for how to appraise body and paint work.)

What kind of a paint job can I expect from one of the quickie-cheapie chain paint places?

Often a surprisingly good job. But *not* good by "good" car-painting definition. Good for the money. For your money you usually get a single coat, which serves as *both* primer and finish, in a choice of *their* colors, not one of them even close to the factory original. And you get it all fast, usually the same day you bring the car in. In by 8:30 A.M., you drive out painted by 5:30 P.M.

You get what one wag calls the "little treatment": a little sanding, a little paint, a little painting—with just a little luck.

But with it all you also get some state-of-the-art advanced technology in quick-production painting. Paint may be specially formulated and even manufactured by the chain. And lots of bright types are at work perfecting the product so that the paint job, as are many, can be warranted.

Whether or not it is a "good" paint job, by definition, begs the question. There is no doubt that, for the money, it is a good cover-up.

How can you lose when a shop, as some of the quick and cheap places do, guarantees the job for up to three years or more against fading?

Insofar as the job fading, you can't. Advanced technology has insured against fading of the paint itself, except in rather rare cases. But you'll notice there is seldom a guarantee against chipping. In effect, the warranties cover the product (the paint), but *not* the application (the painting).

With my original paint wearing, I'd like to have a really good lacquer repainting. Can you paint lacquer over the factory enamel or whatever it was?

One thing it wasn't, for average cars, was

lacquer. And the answer is *no*. Don't attempt (and good shops will not) to paint one type of paint over another. The reason for stripping the car completely to metal is to eliminate the paint-type compatibility problem. Strip it, and you eliminate the problem because you eliminate the old paint.

How long can I expect a paint job to last?

There's really no telling. My kept car has had two good, average paint jobs and neither lasted more than three to four years. Chipping is the main problem. Out of the shop the jobs looked fine. But by the third year out, neither did.

Once you begin painting, you can almost certainly, if you keep the car, figure on painting again.

INTERVIEW:
SECRETS OF A DETAIL MAN
How to Keep Your Car Looking Good — Forever

Mark Cahalane, 27, is a rarity among detail men, the car-keeping artists who generally make the rounds of new and used car dealers. Their special skill: updating the appearance of what the dealer has to sell. With spray can, wax, paint brush, rubbing compound, and consummate automotive artistry, they remove nicks and scratches, burnish rusting chrome to glittering renewed life, make upholstery appear years younger — and tires, with 20,000 miles on their treads, seem slipped just yesterday from the tire maker's mold.

Mark Cahalane is a breed apart. *His* customers — the owners of some of the world's most exotic automobiles and some plainly from middle-class Detroit — *come* to him. His shop, Auto Art, a modest garage behind a storefront in Manhattan Beach, California, deigns even to post a sign out front. Yet here, sometimes alone, sometimes with two assistants, Cahalane works his car-keeping magic. Painstakingly, with a car connoisseur's eye and touch, he keeps his charges — from Ferraris to Fords — looking as good (better, say many of their owners) as the day they came from the factory. When *Car-Keeper's Guide* visited Cahalane, he was at work on perhaps the world's most exotic automobile: a fresh-from-the-factory $95,000 Ferrari 512 Berlinetta Boxer designed by master Italian coachmaker Sergio Pininfarina. Another Pininfarina car — the Cisitalia 202GT, concepted by his late, famous father, Battista — remains the only automobile on permanent display at The New York Museum of Modern Art.

For as little as $40, to $70 and up, a detailer will preen your car to look as good as it possibly can. You take it from there — keeping up its appearance.

Automotive exotics, however, comprise only a part of Cahalane's clientele. The day before *Car-Keeper's Guide*'s visit, he had worked almost as intently in "detailing" a housewife's 1977 Ford LTD. Here, in excerpted interview, he tells some of the ways that car-keepers can keep their cars looking good — perhaps forever.

Cahalane: A car can *always* look new . . . look as good, or better, as the day you bought it *providing* . . . you get to it *before* it begins looking bad.

Q: Ideally, then, car care for car-keepers begins the day an owner takes delivery?

Cahalane: That's the ideal [pointing to the $95,000 Ferrari he's working on, a car with only 360 miles on its odometer, yet *already* in the shop for detailing].

Detailing — sprucing up a car — can do a lot for a car that's been neglected. But the basic idea in detailing, certainly where my clients are concerned, is not restoring a neglected car, or bringing it back as close as possible to its original appearance, although I can do a lot for the appearance of any car. But, rather, to keep a car up so that it *never* looks bad.

Q: Doing that, a car can look good virtually forever?

Cahalane: Absolutely. Ten years down the road it can look very nearly as good as the day you bought it.

Q: And there are some secrets to car care like that?

Cahalane: Actually, more work and knowing how to get on with it than secrets. But there are methods that do the appearance upkeep job right. And wrong ones, which can do a lot of damage.

Q: Obviously, appearance upkeep starts with a wash job?

Cahalane: Yes, with washing it right. Most people start washing their cars from the roof down. That's wrong. You start, for several reasons (one of them being that that's where the dirt really is), at the bottom. With the tires and wheels, before you even wet the rest of the car.

Q: And you use a special wash compound, something you mix with the wash water?

Cahalane: Generally not. You can wash any car with just clear water and nothing more — and do a good job most of the time. Or, if it's really dirty, and road-bugged, use a little Ivory liquid. But *not a detergent* of any kind. We are talking about a soap.

Q: What about most of the wash powders stocked by the auto supply stores?

Cahalane: They're just granulated soap. And the granules, if you're not careful, may not thoroughly mix with the wash water. A good liquid soap does better.

Q: And when do you get around to the car's body itself?

Cahalane: Only after you are through with the tires, the wheels, the bumpers — the dirty, close-to-road parts.

Q: But, of course, most people don't wash their cars. They take them into a quick-wash place.

Cahalane: Never! With one exception: the new *brushless* automatic washers. They are all right.

But the ones that do the wash job with brushes, which includes most of them, are all wrong. They can and do ruin paint jobs. Those stiff, nylon brush bristles rake over a paint job, doing damage, wash by wash. You don't notice the damage after one wash job, or perhaps not even after a dozen. But after a few years you've got scratches that one day will force you to repaint. And that can cost a great deal of money.

Q: So, if you expect to keep your car for a good number of years, and you want to avoid a repainting, you avoid the average car wash places? Either you wash it yourself or have it hand-washed?

Cahalane: Absolutely. And, periodically, every three to four months at least, more often if you have the time, you glaze and wax it.

Q: Glaze it first?

Cahalane: *Before* you wax it, yes. To do it right, to bring up the paint's true, deep color, it's a two-step job. Glaze first, then wax.

Q: Not a one-step job, as most car owners do, using any of the quick, one-step polishing waxes the auto supply stores sell?

Cahalane: No, two steps. To understand why, you need to understand what causes even a car's clean paint to look dull, hazy, and discolored. What causes

When washing car, start with the wheels and dirty lower area. Note, too, how this custom wheel, and raised-letter tires, customize and dress up car.

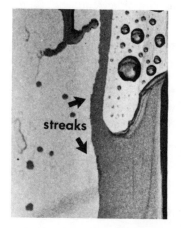 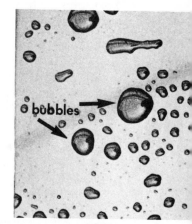

Does the finish need rewaxing? Water pattern on hood gives the answer. Round drops, right, mean wax is all right; streaks, left, indicate need for rewaxing. (Photo courtesy of DuPont Corp.)

it are scratches — minute scratches you can scarcely see. The purpose of the glaze — it's almost like water and usually colorless — is to *fill in* the scratches and bring the color up to where you want it, to where, hopefully, it was right out of the factory.

Q: And then, after the glazing, you wax it?

Cahalane: You must. The glaze simply fills in the scratches and enhances the color. It doesn't protect the paint. In fact, if after glazing, you didn't wax, and you took the car out in the sun, in an hour's time the glaze would be gone — taken right off by sunlight.

Q: So, in effect, waxing protects the glaze first and the finish almost secondarily?

Cahalane: That's right. When you use glaze, as every car owner should, the wax does double duty:

protects the glaze and protects the paint.

Q: Sunlight is to be avoided until you have the wax on it?

Cahalane: Sunlight is to be avoided whenever you're working on a car's finish — when washing, when glazing, when waxing. You work in shade, out of the sun, and at normal room temperature.

Q: Is there a particular type or brand of glaze that seems to work best?

Cahalane: Well, of course, I have my preferences as to brands. But any good industrial-type, hard-finish glaze — available from auto supply stores — is what you want. You put it on with a clean, dry cloth, using a circular motion as you work. And you glaze the entire car before you ever begin wiping it off.

Q: And when, with another clean, soft rag — a diaper, clean T-shirt, or that kind of soft material, you said — you've wiped the glaze off, then you go over it all again, bumper to bumper, with wax?

Cahalane: With 100 percent carnauba wax, nothing less. There are half a dozen or more 100 percent pure carnaubas on the market.

Q: Suppose, as one brand of popular car wax I'm holding in my hand, the container reads, '. . . *with* natural carnauba wax.' Will that do?

Cahalane: No. The 'with' brands won't do, not unless they specify '100 percent carnauba.' When a wax container says 'with,' the question is, 'with *how much* carnauba?' That 'with' tells you, right off, that it is something less, often very much less, than 100 percent carnauba. If it were, it'd say so.

Q: And when you glaze and wax, that includes the chrome?

Cahalane: Yes, the chrome right along with the body paint. And when the wax is dry, you wipe that off, too, with a supersoft cloth — a diaper, cheesecloth, or the like.

Q: But why won't one of the one-step cleaner-waxes work just as well?

Cahalane: For a basic and simple reason. They attempt in one application, because people don't like to take the time for two, and in one formula, because people don't like to spend money for two cans of car polish, to do everything in one step. So they contain a little glaze, a little abrasive cleaner, and a little wax. But not enough of any one of them to do the job right.

Q: So, for someone expecting to keep a car over the years, and keep its appearance up, the two-step is the way to go?

Cahalane: Right. If all you want is a shine, you can get it with a one-step product. But you can't come close to really keeping up the paint job that way over the long haul.

Q: And that's what we're talking about — miles and years more from a paint job?

Cahalane: Exactly. Believe me, if it could be done in just one step, detailers as myself would do it in one.

Q: But suppose there are visible nicks and places

(1) Retouching car's finish: Dab of matched-to-finish retouch paint about to be applied to nick in paint (job was not masked here, but should be).

(2) Retouching car's finish: . . . and, presto! No more paint nick. When retouch spot is dry, it is glazed and waxed along with rest of finish.

where the paint needs touching up? Is that beyond the average non-do-it-yourself owner's skill?

Cahalane: It's within nearly anyone's skill, assuming the places you want to retouch are small. And providing you get a touch-up paint that color-matches what's on the car. Neither is really difficult — either finding a color-matched paint or, once you have it, touching up the spots.

Q: So let's consider the doing — retouching a single, typical little place that needs retouching. Not, of course, a sizable area. *That* calls for repainting, not retouching.

Cahalane: Right. Before you glaze, but after you've washed and dried the car, you dab a little paint — very little on the first try — on the spot. I prefer to use a very small, high-quality artist's brush, *not* the applicator brush that comes with most bottles of retouch paint. It's a good idea, by the way, to mask off (using masking tape) the retouch area. The second step in retouching explains the reason for the masking.

Q: That step comes later?

Cahalane: A full week later. You let the paint dry for a week. Then, remasking if your tape isn't still in place, you carefully, lightly, sand over the spot using very, very fine — say, #600 or so — *wet* sandpaper.

Q: Using very fine wet sandpaper — which is really not a sandpaper, but a super-fine emery paper, usually black in color — is the same technique used, I think, by fine furniture finishers . . . wet-sanding being the secret to achieving a super-smooth finish on furniture?

Cahalane: The same technique, yes.

And after sanding, you rub the retouched place out using rubbing compound, a very fine abrasive that erases any scratches in the retouched place that might have been left by the super-fine wet sandpaper.

Your masking tape, of course, remains in place, the tape being masked in very closely so you can sand and rub out without mistakenly sanding the paint around it — which you don't want to do. Doing that, you'd scratch the body paint.

And, after super-smoothing the retouched place with the rubbing compound, you can glaze and polish the car. That retouched spot will just blend in, the nicked place disappearing as though by magic.

Q: It's as easy as all that?

Cahalane: After a little practice, yes. A car owner might like to try his hand at it first on a nicked place located where it's seldom seen — perhaps way down near the bottom of a rear fender, say, rather than right in the middle of a door.

Q: And retouching a few places this time, another few the next, a car-keeper can gradually gain on his car's paint-missing places. Eventually, he'll get all or most of them retouched.

Cahalane: Yes. The average car owner — unlike professional detailers as ourselves — isn't advised to attempt a total car retouch at one time. Pretty soon the amateur retoucher grows tired and sloppy — and it shows. Do a few retouches today, a few more next week, and finally you'll have the job done.

Q: Until somebody next to your car on a parking lot yanks open a door and slams into it?

Cahalane: Like housecleaning, you never really ever finish with retouching.

Q: What about appearance-izing tires — whether whitewalls or blacks?

Cahalane: To clean whitewalls, assuming they are as curb-marked as most, you need a few simple tools: an old toothbrush for working into the deeper scuff places and one of those not-too-abrasive kitchen scouring pads, plus an all-purpose cleaner. One that I use, though there are many others, is Fantastik, because it comes close to doing that kind of job on whitewall tires.

Q: Suppose there's some black tire rubber area showing in the whitewall area (the whitewall has been abraded away in that area) or, conversely, some whitewall showing in the black tire area?

Cahalane: You touch out the intruding white with flat, black paint where black is supposed to be or with white, in a tire-intruded whitewall area. In both cases, model airplane enamel works well. Touchouts of tire walls, black or white, make a big difference.

Q: What about de-dingying black wall tires or any black tire area?

Cahalane: Except for touching out those white or black intrusion places, what you *don't* do is paint over any rubber or vinyl surfaces, though some detailers on the car lots do, as you've probably noticed.

Q: Painting tires, as some used-lot detailers do, is one of those drive-out jobs — a job intended to last just long enough for somebody to buy the car and drive it out?

Cahalane: Exactly. But we're talking about long-term appearance maintenance.

What brings out the *original* color — whether black on tires, a vinyl top's color, the once good looks of a vinyl or plastic dashboard, or even the color in rubber or plastic molding is a polypenetrant.

Q: One of the store-available spray-on/rub-off formulas that penetrate and also gloss the surface?

Cahalane: That does both, yes. There are a number of good polypenetrants, including *Armor All,* the one I usually use, Poly-Guard, STP's Son of A Gun, and some others.

Q: And besides whatever else they do, they also

To bring tire's black up to new tire sheen, detailer Mark Cahalane uses polypenetrant, such as Armor All.

protect a surface against sunlight, the sun's ultra-violet rays?

Cahalane: Yes. Nearly all of the polypenetrants not only bring up the original color, penetrate the material and put a sheen on things, but also act as a sunscreen. They shield sunlight, which saps the color in vinyl tops, in rubber molding, and in tires.''

Q: What about the bothersome upkeep problem with car chrome — a major appearance problem for many who keep their cars longer?

Cahalane: Well, probably any good chrome cleaner will handle *well-kept* chrome — chrome that has merely lost its luster. But where rusting is involved, you've got a different problem and you use a different technique.

Q: The chrome cleaners can't handle rust in chrome?

Cahalane: Not as well as some other products and techniques, although a really badly rusted chrome area doesn't handle all that well by any method. If it's that badly corroded, the chrome simply is no longer there.

Q: Which is another good reason for keeping up a car — and its chrome — from the start?

Cahalane: Among the very best reasons, proving again that to keep it looking good you can never permit it really to look bad. If, from the start, you glaze and wax chrome and do it regularly, rusting is slowed to a crawl and may often be prevented altogether, depending on where you live and drive.

Q: In working over rust places in chrome, do you still use that toothbrush to get into the crevices?

Cahalane: Sometimes. We use, as you've noticed, a toothbrush in a number of our detailing techniques.

But the key to getting rid of chrome rust is to use a weak acid on it. And with the acid, very, very light steel wool. The rust-removing weak acid I prefer is naval jelly.

You rub over the rusted place with the naval jelly, then work the area over with the steel wool. It works very well.

Q: And after you've used the acid and steel wool, and have cleaned away as much of the rust as possible from bumpers, grilles, headlight covers, trim, and other chromed parts, you rinse away the acid with water?

Cahalane: Right. Then dry the area. And then do to the chrome what you did to the car's painted surfaces: glaze and wax it.

Q: Have you a prime example showing what good detailing, as you've described it, can accomplish in reviving even a long neglected car's appearance?

Cahalane [grinning and pointing to a gleaming, 10-year-old two-door Datsun 510 parked nearby]: My own car, which I picked up about a year ago for $1,250. Every square inch of its body paint is the original factory paint. But when I bought it, it was shot-looking. Terrible. I could see, however, that with proper detailing and attention to details, I could bring that Datsun, sun-faded original paint and all, back to close to what it had been when new.

Q: But it wasn't an easy thing?

Cahalane: Careful detailing never is. It takes time, but it is time well spent. And it is one do-it-yourself job any car owner can do.

Q: As a car-keeper yourself, was the time you invested in detailing your own decade-old Datsun really worth it, other than for appearance's sake?

Cahalane [grinning]: Well, the other day I was offered twice what I paid for the car.

YEARS-LONGER STRATEGY: EXTERIOR

1. Avoid parking beneath finish-endangering trees. If sap, acidic bird droppings, or other finish ruiners splatter finish, remove them as soon as you discover them with a generous water rinse (and nonalkaline mild soap suds, if stubborn).
2. Have it hand-washed or patronize only *brushless* car wash places.
3. Maintain its sun- and fade-resistant waxed finish, winter and summer.
4. Clean chrome often enough to avoid rusting, then protect chrome with identical-to-finish treatment: first a glaze coat, then a wax coat.
5. Touch up or have touched up nicks and rock bruises, especially any that go to the primer or to bare metal, to avoid rusting.
6. Do whatever you have to do to avoid repainting. Nothing within financial reason duplicates the original factory paint job.

Chapter 15: Interior
Give It the Red Carpet Treatment

No matter how long-kept their cars, some few—a fortunate few million or so car-keepers—give scant heed to the growing-old-without-grace interiors of their cars.

They don't care because, living within easy driving distance of Mexico and its border towns (Mexicali, Tijuana, Nogales, Ciudad Juarez, Nuevo Laredo, and others), they periodically head south of the border. And there, in sometimes nondescript car-redo and upholstery shops, they buy some of the last automotive interior bargains available anywhere. And with them, usually excellent materials (imported American and European interior fabrics) and, at the better places, rare craftsmanship. Invariably, the border car craftsmen start from scratch—with a bolt of vinyl, car cloth, or a run of leather. A few hours and thousands of machine stitches later, they have crafted, at about one-third the price you'd pay stateside, car interiors to suit any owner's fancy: luxuriously customized or plain jane.

You can have your car completely recarpeted for $50–$60; a new headliner (ceiling) installed for about the same price or less; roll-and-tuck vinyl seatcovers, front and back, for around $100; and every interior door panel redone as good as new for seldom more than $75.

You are expected to bargain hard before a final price is agreed upon (often 25–40 percent less than the upholsterer's original asking price). And you would do well, once you have selected from his book of vinyl or cloth swatches the color and texture you want, to make sure that the material you get is the same thickness (gauge) as the swatch book's sample. Often, it is something considerably less. Insist that you get what you bargained for.

Not many car-keepers have the advantage of proximity—as do southern Californians, some Arizonians and New Mexicans, Texans, south and west, and car owners in other near-Mexico states.

For the rest of us, as indeed for even the border-jumpers, there is an abiding single rule for keeping a car's interior new: *To keep it up, never let it get down.*

And while any spruce-up place will houseclean your car's growing-drab interior for anywhere from $25 to $75, most car-keepers, while shopping out virtually every other job, tend their car's interior themselves.

Says the owner of a whistling-clean 1978 Buick Riviera, from Indianapolis, Indiana, "I make car cleaning just an extension of housecleaning. I've got the vacuum out anyway, and the spray-on can of rug shampoo, and window cleaner."

So natural a progression, house to car,

triggers an intriguing question. "If household cleaning aids—from rug shampoo to vinyl cleaner—work in the house, why don't they work in the car?"

They do, though a survey of shelf after shelf of so-called "automobile" products at any auto supply store would lead you to believe otherwise: that there's something special and sacrosanct about what cleans a car's interior and what cleans a home's interior.

Generally, there is nothing all that special except for the price and label, which almost always pictures an automobile, about the "automotive" products the auto store sells. What's special is the marketing. For product makers, there can be enormous "double-selling" by convincing drivers that their home carpet cleaner won't clean the car carpet.

Of course it will. Carpet is carpet, even though the one never budges from the floor while the other sometimes travels at better than 55 mph.

If you were a maker of rug shampoo, and if you could clean up in four markets merely by switching labels, hawking one as "household carpet shampoo," another as "executive suite shampoo" (for the office), a third as "mobile home shampoo," and yet a fourth as "auto carpet shampoo," you surely would—and fire your marketing director if he didn't. That is what marketing is all about: segmenting the market.

None of this means that you'll always get the best with housecleaning products, however. On the auto store's shelves are, in fact, some very excellent interior car-cleaning products that are seldom duplicated in your home's broom closet. These products aren't often found at home because most housecleaners would find them useful only now and then, while the car owner has almost everyday use for them.

Products used on a car's exterior—and to some extent in its interior—also have to stand up reasonably well under environmental conditions not common to your living room or mine. Rain, snow, freezing (car interiors get winter chill), and heat—sometimes oven heat if a car's parked in summer's 100° F. sunshine with its windows closed—are some elements your car is probably exposed to. Nor does the average living room carpet, sun-shielded by blinds or drapes, lie as naked to sunlight and its fabric-fading ultraviolet rays as does your car.

A car is also exposed—unlike most home interiors—to road-blown dust, exhaust smog, and fumes from its own engine compartment. And should its occupants smoke in a closed car, eventually cigarette smoke tints and grimes windows and vinyl.

Nonetheless, granted even that some auto interior products do a multitude of jobs well—brighten tire sidewalls, vinyl tops, interior vinyl, and even the padded dash—what's in your broom closet will also likely do almost all of these things. And, when it comes to a car's interior, they will do them as well.

Household products, moreover—for many car owners—have the added advantage of familiarity. You know what they will or will not do well. You are far less familiar with many of the car-cleaning products even when they may be identical to what you use at home. For their labels, generally, are not.

What of the almost universal claim by auto interior cleaning products—whether pour-on, spray-on, rub-off, or glaze-over—that they will somehow take all the work out of car cleaning? Their no-work guarantees are clearly overstated. Nothing gets your interior car upkeep job done but you. No amount of canned goods really makes it all that much easier or less time-consuming.

So let's set to work keeping up your car's interior. And while we're about it, let's name just a few of the auto products available, in addition to what you already have at home, to help you get on with the job.

Upholstery (Cloth, Vinyl, Leather)

Keep-clean methods for car cloth (called "fabric-type trim" by some auto makers), vinyl, and leather upholstery are all different, but each is relatively simple.

What is *not* simple is the first step in upholstery upkeep: emergency cleaning. You must immediately take care of emergencies right after they happen, should something stain, gum, spot, or otherwise taint the upholstery. Says a car interior expert, "If you don't get to these emergencies right away, the sooner the better, the battle is lost." He is referring to permanent stains, which unless speedily removed, will stay with the upholstery the rest of its road life.

General Motors, for one, dealer-stocks three general-purpose cleaning products that are also compounded for emergency cleanup:

For Car-Cloth (Fabric-Type Trim):

GM Fabric Cleaner, a solvent-type general-purpose and spot cleaner, also for emergency spot lifting. It should be used only in a well-ventilated car (doors and windows wide open).

GM Multi-Purpose Powdered Cleaner, dispensed as a foam, both for general

Vinyl cracks such as these can often be prevented by regular use of a penetrant/protectant vinyl conditioner and brightener.

cleanup and to use after the solvent in emergency rehabilitation.

For Vinyl

GM Vinyl Cleaner, generally reserved for emergency cleanup of vinyl upholstery, door panels, armrests, and other vinyl car covering.

Here, drawn in part from various GM Owner's Manuals, are the car-keeper's hopeful quick cures for some of the everyday worst emergencies that can befall an auto interior—emergencies that threaten permanently to despoil interior good looks, even upholstery life, unless quickly gotten to. Similar non-GM products, both home and auto types, may do as well.

Handling Car-Cloth Upholstery Emergencies

For *general* stain removal on car cloth upholstery (we'll list special-case emergency stains and their slightly different treatment later), first *carefully* scrape off the excess stain, using a dull knife. Or blot it up with a paper towel. Then remove the stain with GM Fabric Cleaner or a similar product.

In the removal process, a clean cheesecloth wetted (never soaked) with the fabric cleaner works best.

One important point to remember about all in-car *fabrics,* contrasted to vinyls: fabrics should not be overwetted. The idea is not to penetrate the fabric any deeper than necessary. Soak the fabric, and you may have created another problem (mildew).

With the cheesecloth or a clean rag moistened with the fabric cleaner, *begin* at the *outside* of the stain and work *toward the center,* "feathering" the cleaning toward the center, as you go. Change to a clean cloth or a clean area of the cloth as you work.

Once the stain is cleaned from the fabric, *immediately* dry the stain area, using any *force-dry* method readily at hand: heat lamp, hair dryer, or compressed air (for the latter, you'll likely have to drive to a service station). Use caution, of course, not to burn the fabric in the process of drying it. What you're aiming for, obviously, is to prevent a cleaning ring.

If a ring should form, *immediately* repeat the cleaning process, only over a slightly larger area. Again, feather the cleaning inward, from the now larger area toward the center.

This may seem opposite from household stain removal methods where feathering—using an ever softer, lighter touch—is often done from the center outward. The other way around usually works better for auto fabric de-ringing.

Finally, if a ring, even though scarcely discernible, remains, do one final treatment: repeat once again, but this time mask off a larger fabric area. Clean a full-fabric section, seam-to-seam, which includes the still lingering ring. And this time use only the *suds* (not the liquid) of the GM Fabric Cleaner or another good fabric cleaner, applying with a clean sponge or *soft* brush. That, hopefully, should get rid of the most usual ("general") stains on fabrics.

Special-Case Emergency Stains on Car Fabrics

Grease/oil/tar/greasy stains, as from suntan oil, peanut butter, mayonnaise, butter, margarine, shoe polish, chewing gum, wax crayons, coffee *with cream,* and other greasy products should be treated as for general stains. But, in handling greasy stains, as well as ink and lipstick, *do not enlarge the stain area.* And with ink and some lipsticks, hope for the best. A number of them defy complete removal. That's the reason for the warning not to enlarge their stain area. You may spread the ink, lipstick, or grease and make matters far worse.

Nongreasy stains, including fruit juices, milk, soft drinks, wine, catsup, black coffee, and blood, vomit, or urine. Treat as for general stains, but, in the final suds-only process (the suds from either a good fabric detergent or, typically, GM's Fabric Cleaner), use the suds cool.

In the case of urine or vomit, if odor persists, before you force-air-dry the stain area, very lightly apply a cool or lukewarm solution made from water and baking soda.

The anti-odor solution formula: 1 teaspoon of baking soda to 1 cup of water.

Routine Car Fabric Upkeep

First vacuum, whisk broom, or wipe the fabric clean with a clean cloth. Then, with a clean sponge or *soft* bristled brush, apply any of the ready-mix or mix-it-yourself car fabric cleaners—among them the GM Fabric Cleaner (in this case, mixed with water, as label-directed). Or use such fabric cleaners as Simoniz Car Interior Cleaner, most good household detergents, and Woolite, often used to clean sweaters and other delicates. A very weak water and ammonia solution is often good, too, for routine fabric cleaning.

The ammonia-water formula (which also does a good window cleaning job): 4–6 tablespoons of ammonia to 1 quart of water.

Whatever the fabric cleaner—name-brand or no-name (generic, as ammonia)—test it first. Try a small area of the fabric that normally isn't in view. If what's happening doesn't look right (you detect fading or a tint of fabric color shows on your cloth), stop right there. Let things dry. Regroup: wait a day. And test another fabric cleaner or its water-based mix.

Car cloth upholstery, obviously, is the most difficult type of interior fabric to keep clean or to clean after it becomes dirty or stained. That's one reason why car-cleaning professionals charge more to clean the interior of a fabric-upholstered car.

In fabric care and cleaning, patience is its own reward. The gotta-do-it-today syndrome has aged even more a lot of aging car fabric, showing up sun fade where an owner didn't suspect it existed, causing streaks and revealing, as most would prefer them not revealed, wear-and-tear places.

No, the job does *not* have to be done today. Far better to test, observe the results when dry, and then proceed tomorrow or the day after. General car-fabric cleaning (as contrasted to emergency cleanup) can, like housework, be put off. And even "car company" isn't apt to notice. They will, however, if the cleaning job is botched.

Going a long way toward protecting car fabrics against emergency as well as routine cleanup is the *Scotchgard* treatment, or similar products, long used on home upholstery. *But,* Scotchgarding is recommended only for *new* car upholstery, not for old, faded, or long-used fabric. For new cars, or for the newly reupholstered, have the fabric treated immediately by the dealer or upholsterer or do it yourself. Scotchgard, Turtle Wax's Polyshell Fabric Upholstery Protection, and others come in spray cans.

Cleaning Vinyl Car Upholstery

Even though some of today's car vinyls seem not to be as long-lived or as fade-resistant as those just a few years ago, an appraisal their makers would debate, vinyl is a snap to clean. But it is not necessarily easy to *keep* clean.

There's a difference. Vinyl upholstery and other in-car vinyls clean easily. Soap and warm water, the soap the nonalkaline type, does it. But vinyl seems to get grimier faster. Or, at least the grime is more noticeable.

There's really no reason to buy a vinyl product that just cleans, when no-cost soap and water will do. But, unless you are very careful, rinse the vinyl well and wipe dry, soap can dull and streak vinyl. There are a number of vinyl cleaning products on the market, however, formulated not merely to clean but to *sheen* vinyl. A few among the many: J Wax Vinyl Top & Interior Cleaner, Turtle Wax Vinyl Plus, Mopar Leather and Vinyl Cleaner (available at Chrysler company dealerships), Tuff Stuff (a Union Carbide product), and others.

Many interior pros, the so-called detail men, favor Armor All, a polymer-based protectant/penetrant, which brings up the color in vinyl, gives it a sheen, and helps

Leather-look (because it's real leather) looks and feels good and is among the easiest of interiors to keep looking that way. (Photo courtesy of Cadillac, Div. of General Motors.)

protect against sun fading. But the product—three spray-on/rub-off applications over two to three days are recommended—is not a cleaner. Before using this, or several other penetrant-type vinyl reconditioners, the vinyl must be cleaned either with vinyl cleaner or with soap and water.

While there is little dispute that Armor All is one of the better car-keeping products (but it should *not* be used on fabric upholstery), it sometimes tends to make vinyl upholstery slippery, Its formulators say this happens when users apply an overdose—too thick or too many applications in too short a time. Usually, a little buffing with a clean cloth will deslick the vinyl surface.

Cleaning Leather

Many of the fabric and vinyl cleaners very definitely should not be used on leather—real leather, as contrasted to looks-like-leather vinyl. If your upholstery is leather, you know it and are not likely to take it for its imitators.

Saddle soap and water, obviously, do a good job of cleaning and dressing in-car leather, just as saddle soap has done for years on boots, leather shoes, and saddles.

In its owner manual, Mercedes-Benz, whose clientele is prone to leather, recommends nothing but wiping its leather upholstery with a damp cloth, then drying thoroughly. Mercedes cautions, however, that when cleaning perforated leather, you should avoid permitting the leather's underside to become wet.

Carpeting

What cleans your home carpets cleans your car's. That includes virtually any of the spray-on/bristle brush/rub-on foam carpet shampoos.

Before or after vacuuming (most experts say *before*), car carpeting should be rid of spots. Use a prespotting household cleaner. Follow this with a detergent wash. Then use a rug shampoo.

If you have a tank-type home vacuum with an upholstery fitting, trundle it out to the garage. Don't waste time or money on those plug-into-the-cigarette-lighter car vacuums. They are long on looks but short on performance.

If what's on the carpet is grease, tar, or the like, use a solvent-type cleaner (such as General Motor's). If road-salted snow or slush not only whitens or greys the carpet but, in melting, stains it, do this: First, brush away what snow and slush you can. Then vacuum up what remains. If the stain persists, it can. often be removed with a carefully applied saltwater solution.

Snow stain spot removal formula: 1 cup of table salt to 1 quart of water.

Now finish the snow cleanup job with a foamy carpet shampoo.

Cleaning Hard-to-Reach Places

Car designers are forever "crevicing": creating, as if by design, in-car crevices that are difficult, sometimes nearly impossible, to reach and clean even with a home vacuum's long-nosed upholstery attachment.

One such place is the meeting of dashboard and windshield. On some cars it becomes an unsightly graveyard for bugs. If you can't vacuum them out, perhaps because your vacuum or its fitting won't reach, try air-blowing them out. What does it is an aerosol spray—Dust Off is one such product—that, though meant to clean delicate camera innards and the spaces between typewriter keys, works for car crevices just as well. Most camera and stereo stores stock the aerosol air sprays.

Cleaning/Sheening Dashboard and Instrument Panels

Aside from periodically dusting the dash or wiping over it with a chemically impregnated polishing cloth (Magna Cloth is one of this genre), the vinyl penetrants are the number one choice for renewing the appearance, no matter how sun-faded, of dashboard vinyl and plastic. Again, use the likes of Armor All, Poly-Guard, STP's Son of A Gun, or others available in auto stores and supermarkets.

Moldings (Vinyl, Rubber, Composition)

Door and window moldings need to be tended not just to revitalize their color (though most are black), but to keep them flexible and functioning. Their function, of course, is to seal out rain, snow, dust, cold, and road noise. After a while, moldings grow hard and brittle.

What keeps them pliable and their color up are any of the polypenetrants (again, Poly-Guard, Armor All, etc.). But silicone-based molding rejuvenators are sometimes preferred, mainly because they seem to keep moldings more flexibly alive than do the poly-based, even though the poly spray-ons do a better job of restoring the color of moldings.

Repairing Ripped, Cracked, Worn Vinyl

Despite a dozen products meant to repair rips in vinyl upholstery, patch over that hole in the car's carpet, and repair cracks in window moldings or even the dash, don't hoist your expectations too high.

Some work—to a point. None, except occasionally in the hands of a pro interior or detail man, totally masks the wear or damage.

Where the vinyl menders, in particular,

fail is at the very places they're needed most: at upholstery stress points, notably the driver's seat and seat back. They wear and rip first because someone is always in the driver's seat, so that's where a car's greatest upholstery stress areas are. After miles and months stress takes its toll.

You could hardly expect a patch, or the bonding of a rip's edges with vinyl glue, to withstand the stress the original fabric could not. Patching or gluing rips in driver seat vinyl simply doesn't work.

If there were easy fixes for vinyl seat rips, we'd mention them. Or, put another way, there are *easy* fixes, but no *satisfactory* fixes, except reupholstery.

Window/Windshield Interiors

The interior side of car glass is often neglected because it's hard to reach and clean without risking soaking the upholstery and because doing it is usually awkward and cramped. But there's really no sense in washing them on the outside when the insides are dirty.

Any home window cleaner (spray-on/wipe-on/rub-on) works, but a mild ammonia or vinegar solution works best.

Ammonia or vinegar window cleaning formula: 4 tablespoons of either to 1 quart of water.

Nonetheless, interior window/windshield washing can be a bug. Not that there are many bugs on the inside of the pane, just that to get the inside *really* clean isn't one of those three-minute car chores.

A small squeegee helps to wipe down the excess ammonia or vinegar cleaning solution. But protect bottom window molding and upholstery with a little dam of paper towels. And wipe the squeegee rubber dry after each sweep of the pane. Clean, lint-free paper towels get into the corners (where the squeegee can't), and finish the job.

So you have perhaps ten minutes to spare and figure you'll give the car's interior a thorough cleaning?

Oh, no, you won't! Tending the kept car's—or any car's—interior simply isn't a chore that can be done all that quickly.

YEARS-LONGER STRATEGY: INTERIOR

1. Protect the car interior against sun-fade. Park in the shade whenever you can.
2. If something stains carpeting or upholstery, clean it up immediately, before it dries. Waiting even an hour may leave a permanent stain.
3. If you have the car seats reupholstered, make very sure that the fabric or vinyl is top quality, thus likely less fade-prone. Always have new fabric upholstery treated with a fabric protector (such as Scotchgard), or spray it yourself.
4. Use a driver's seat cushion to reduce upholstery stress. Stress-point rips and tears can be prevented for years.
5. Pets — especially dogs — can turn a car interior doggy in no time. The choice is yours: your pet or the upholstery.
6. Make car cleaning just another housecleaning chore.

Chapter 16: Maintenance
Maintaining It Right

"Those self-service stations are killing off a whole generation of cars," declares an observer on the automotive scene. While perhaps *not* the whole generation, enough of it to make you brake hard and stop to think: did you even so much as look under the hood the last time—or the last six times—you self-served at the bargain no-service gas places?

Chances are you didn't. Neither do most other self-service car owners. Some of them are losing batteries (from failure to check their water levels), tires (through inflation neglect), and, far worse, engines (through lack of oil).

In these days of dizzying fuel prices, any car-keeper appreciates a self-service bargain. But is 20¢ saved on a gallon really worth spending $750–$1,000 for a new engine?

You can still save that 20¢ and not spend that $750–$1,000 simply by patronizing a full-service station every other refill or so or by making sure, when self-servicing, also to self-service what's under the hood, under the fenders (the tires), and underfoot (the transmission).

How does the car-keeper maintain it right? Comprising this chapter and, you will have noticed, appropriately appearing elsewhere in the text are two guides designed to help you do (or have done) routine car-keeping maintenance. And, should something other than routine develop, consider the symptoms and their possible causes.

Years-Longer Strategy

Although these do-it-right routine maintenance guides simplify the routine of keeping a car longer, they go beyond the routine. Each of the maintenance strategies is designed, whatever the component involved, to stretch out the road life of that component into the foreseeable future or

Dot reminder stuck to door edge reminds self-service car-keeper the car needs full servicing, not just a fill-up.

129

however long you intend, or now plan, to keep your car.

As more than simply maintenance ABCs, each is meant to advance your personal car-keeping strategy. And, in fact, to make car-keeping practical and possible over the years.

No guide, nor any single strategy, can fit every make, model, and year of car on the road. Certainly, as a supplement, you should check each maintenance prescription against what your owner's manual may also prescribe for that particular component or automotive function. Where there is a *significant* divergence between a guide and the recommendation of your owner's manual, heed the manual's.

But, the maintenance guides in this book are specially formulated for the owner who wants to keep a car longer. The guides tend to prescribe *more* maintenance, not less. Some owner's manuals tend, by contrast, to err on the side of infrequency. They do because they prefer not to burden car buyers with upkeep chores, or with "having to look after" their cars, or worse: with the notion that, if a car needs more maintenance more frequently, it must somehow be either a mechanical misfit or a highway prima donna.

For one example, nearly all auto makers are attempting to stretch out the miles between engine oil changes. To do so is more convenient and less costly for car buyers.

To accommodate the maintenance lazy, most owner's manuals in effect prescribe *two* mileage intervals for changing oil in a particular maker's engine. One is labeled, if it is labeled at all, as the "normal" oil-change mileage interval, which is really the buyer-convenience stretch-out interval. The other, sometimes hidden away in small print, is labeled the "severe" mileage interval between oil changes—a mileage and time interval that may be *half* that of the "normal."

If you drive in stop-and-go town traffic, and if most of your driving, whatever the traffic, is short-distance and shuttle-run, to your engine you do "severe" driving.

Most of the years-longer strategies are

Small car small engines work far harder than bigger engines, and their smaller oil filters (left) simply cannot be neglected. When you change the oil, change the filter. (Photo courtesy of Fram Corporation.)

based on what today is "normal" for most cars: "severe" driving.

Maintain your car by "severe" mileage intervals, at slightly more cost, admittedly, and you will effectively stretch out the miles and years before major component maintenance is necessary.

An ironclad guarantee? No, it is not, nor can it be. What is all but guaranteed, however, is that following "normal" maintenance intervals, you'll be visiting your mechanic far sooner and far more frequently.

Symptoms/Causes

These guides, likewise appearing throughout the text, are designed to alert you to symptoms that, if heeded, may help you head off or reduce major maintenance over the miles and years.

Some of the guides' symptoms you may already be familiar with—as well as with their possible causes. Others you may not.

Again, no symptom/possible cause listing is infallible. Cars are growing more complex. And for increasing numbers of '80s cars (those with advanced electronic systems), yesterday's "possible cause"—such as a malfunctioning carburetor—may no longer even exist under the hood.

On the other hand, a symptom may point to pending maintenance or, as readily, to bad driving habits. If so, both the possible mechanical fault and the possible human fault, which may cause or mask the real problem, are listed.

Another important use for the Symptoms/Causes guides is to forearm you in dealing with mechanics and shopmen. With a Symptoms/Causes guide in hand, you need to know nothing about a particular component to be able to ask the questions any car-keeper should be able to ask a mechanic.

Nonetheless, the symptoms guides aren't intended to make you a mechanic, merely a more informed car-keeper. Usually, only the more usual possible causes for any symptom are shown. The more unusual are beyond the scope or purpose of this book.

For your referral and quick reference, all of the Symptoms/Causes guides and Years-Longer Strategy guides are listed in the index.

Having read this far, you know—as only an insider can know—the ins and outs of car-keeping. And, possibly, more about your car than you had known before. Or, perhaps, more than you really thought you wanted to know.

But now you know . . .

. . . how brakes work and what the mechanic means when he tells you he's going to replace their *pads* or *linings*. You know, should you ever face a major engine decision, your options—and what they involve.

. . . where and how to get the work done, how to shop it out, and how to find, wherever you live, not merely a good mechanic, but a supermechanic. You know how to size up—as indicative of the job you can expect—a body shop's work in progress. And you know the difference between a good paint job and something far less.

You know what every car-keeper needs to know: how to make your car last years longer—or for just as long as you want it to last.

CHECKLIST OF
ROUTINE MAINTENANCE NEGLECT

"Incredible!" is how one car expert summed it up.

He had just read a road survey conducted by the American Automobile Association (AAA), which showed that nearly 80 percent of some 237 cars, checked by the auto club, suffered from "routine maintenance neglect." That means neglect of routine little things that anyone who drives, and most especially anyone who wants to keep a car longer, is expected routinely to look after or have looked after.

In checking those randomly sampled 237 cars, the AAA found this:

- 34 percent low a quart or more on oil
- 31 percent low on radiator coolant
- 28 percent low on antifreeze
- 27 percent low on windshield washer solvent
- 22 percent with improper tire pressure
- 13 percent low on power steering fluid
- 11 percent low on battery fluid

- 5 percent with loose or frayed fan belts
- 5 percent with defective lights or turn signals
- 4 percent with an unusable spare tire (or none)
- 3 percent low on brake fluid

Neglect of *safety items* is even more widespread, finds another recent survey, this one by the Motor and Equipment Manufacturers Association (MEMA).

A MEMA car check of cars whose ages averaged 3.86 years showed that nearly 54 percent had never, over nearly four years and considerable mileage, had their brakes repaired. And 57.7 percent were still being driven with their original shock absorbers, even though shock absorber life is seldom longer than two years or about 25,000 miles.

Plainly, for car-keepers, this is no way to keep a car — nor to keep it operating safely.

SLEUTHING DRIVEWAY DRIPS

One thing the 21st century's space driver need never worry about: driveway drip. In the absence of Earthbound gravity, nothing drips.

But on today's driveways, ruled by Earth's gravity, drips cause some car-keepers to go into orbit insofar as their equilibrium is concerned.

"It's leaking oil!" a car owner tells her husband. "I'd better take it right in to see what's wrong."

Possibly, nothing is wrong. Or, if wrong, it's not all that wrong. The drip may not even be oil. It could be coolant, overflowing the car's pressurized radiator after a particularly long and heated drive. It might be the air conditioner's condenser cooling off and dripping condensate: water. Or it might be something that really does deserve a mechanic's look.

Virtually all cars now and then drip a little. Older cars tend to drip more. And while it is a truism, the older the car, seemingly the more it drips. Nonetheless, there is only occasional reason for any quick alarm.

First, do a little sleuthing. Determine what the drip is and, if possible and easy, where it might be dripping from. In most cars, there are only a half dozen fluids that can drip:

Water

Water could be from the air conditioner, after it's been on and you've turned it off. Or, upon first starting up in the morning — and sometimes even before — some water may puddle from the tailpipe. Overnight, moisture often condenses and collects in the tailpipe. No matter; water is water and readily identifiable. Dab a finger into the drip spot and sniff it for any nonwater smell. At the very least, if it isn't water, you'll know so instantly.

Radiator Coolant

This is the "water" that most often drips, and occasionally gushes, from a car. Generally, it's only about 50 percent water. The rest is a slippery, glycerinlike antifreeze/antirust inhibitor (most likely ethylene glycol), which gives the coolant water its slightly chemical smell and slippery feel.

Of course, if you don't keep coolant in your radiator (you *always should!*), what leaks out, if it leaks, is water — 100 percent. And that tends to complicate the sleuthing.

The single most leak-prone, and thus drip-prone, areas of any car involve its cooling system. Radiators, scarcely really improved in years, spring leaks — especially since they are under considerably higher pressure than in years past. The water pump, on the engine's front, can leak. When it does, there's seldom any mistaking where *that* leak is coming from. The top and bottom radiator hoses, as well as

the usual two that go to the car's interior heater, periodically leak, unless you have them changed every year or so or when they look or feel as if they are growing weak.

A frayed, worn look is obvious. If a radiator hose, when you squeeze it, is either very flabby or brittle, it is likely, too, in need of replacement. When a radiator hose spurts a leak it is likely to be the largest leak any driver ever observes in his or her car. There's water everywhere but where it is supposed to be — in the radiator.

Sometimes, however, what appears to be a hose leak where a radiator hose, especially the top one, is clamped around the cast-iron or aluminum hose fitting on the engine is something else. What has happened is that electrolysis — a tiny electrical current — has eaten a hole right through the metal. What has to be replaced to stop the leak is the fitting and possibly not the hose.

Water — whether dripping or gushing — is always a concern because if it's coolant, eventually (and sometimes far sooner) your radiator will have so little water that it'll boil. And you'll be stopped.

Actually, the more worrisome sign of water is almost constant *white smoke* coming out of the tailpipe long after the engine has warmed up. It can signal an internal engine coolant-water leak — for radiator coolant circulates all through the inner engine to prevent it from burning itself up.

Transmission/Torque Converter/ Power Steering Fluid

If the driveway drip spot is red or reasonably red, it is almost certainly from the transmission, its torque converter, or the power steering system. Makers of transmission and power steering fluid color-code it red so the mechanic can easily identify its source.

A transmission fluid leak, which comes from an area in most cars near the rear of the engine, can mean only a worn transmission pan gasket. Or it might indicate that the transmission needs routine maintenance — something every owner should see it gets, anyway. But if the red fluid drip seems to be coming from near the front of the engine — on many cars from the left side (the driver's side) — it may be coming from the power steering, in particular the reservoir in which the power steering rotor spins. It could mean a crack in that unit. If so, the unit will have to be replaced. Or, if you've just had the car in for servicing, it could merely mean that the reservoir has been overfilled.

Grease

Grease, used to lubricate gears, the car's grease

fittings (greased routinely when a car is lubed) and reservoired in considerable quantity in the rear end differential gearing, is unmistakable. It looks like oil but is far thicker.

After your car has been lubed it may drip a little grease for a few days. This is because when the lube man "shot" the car's lube fittings with grease, some accumulated on the fittings. And it drips.

While it happens, cars generally don't for very long drip grease — mainly because grease isn't really drippy, and unless there's a crack in a major grease reservoir, as the differential (highly unusual), there really aren't all that many places for grease to drip from.

Gasoline

There's no mistaking a gasoline drip. And no mistaking that it's nothing to put off having a mechanic investigate. It could be a fuel pump leak, a fuel line leak, or more dangerous, if possible, even than these, a gas tank leak.

Diesel Fuel

If yours is a diesel-engined car, diesel fuel can leak from a number of places, including the fuel tank, fuel lines, fuel fittings, or the fuel injection system, which is under high pressure. Happily, diesel fuel under normal conditions is not explosive. It only becomes so when atomized within the diesel engine. Diesel fuel is unmistakable because, well, it smells like diesel fuel, which is to say like kerosene, a smell many diesel owners don't particularly cherish.

Oil

We've saved the most frequent drip for the last. It is also often the hardest to locate. There are dozens of places in a car from which oil may drip. To name but a few: the oil filter, the engine oil reservoir and its pan, any number of engine oil seals and gaskets that are there, among other reasons, to prevent oil leaks, and various other places where oil is confined under pressure.

Your car may burn gasoline, but it runs on oil.

A common cause of oil drips is a loose or thread-stripped oil filter, which contains upwards of a quart of oil. What happens is that when the lube man screws in a new filter he either doesn't properly tighten it or he gets it in crooked, stripping its threads and permitting oil to leak.

One trouble with oil leaks, especially, is that mechanics seem to have a hard time finding their precise origins. While they guess and "by-gosh," they're costing you money.

When you bring your car in with an oil leak that seems to come from the rear of the engine, the easiest and among the costliest jobs the mechanic can suggest is installing a new *main rear engine seal.* Figuring his time, his trouble, and the seal, you can expect a bill for $80–$100.

Actually, such a snap decision is often patently dishonest — or sloppy — as too often you discover when, bill paid, oil continues to drip, unabated, as before.

The problem is that engine oil leaks are plain sneaky. The older the kept car, the sneakier they seem. Reason: after a number of miles and years, unless you keep your engine factory clean, a residue of oil builds beneath most engines. It effectively conceals where the leak *is* and even where the leak might be *coming* from.

There's one solution: a solution of solvents, perhaps also along with steam cleaning, to clean away all the gunk.

If the mechanic does the job right, after cleaning the underengine he dries it. Then, with the engine going, he carefully observes its now clean underside for signs of oil runs or drips. Unless he does that, he cannot know for sure from where an oil leak, which appears on a dirty engine to be a rear engine leak, is really coming from.

Very often an oil drip that appears to be coming from the rear of an engine, because that's where it's dripping oil, isn't coming from the engine's rear at all. Rather, it's coming from worn gaskets on top and at the front of the engine, which are supposed to seal the engine's head and valve covers. Since many engines are installed on a slight slant, any oil drip from up front, especially from the top of the engine, runs down the engine's "rails" and eventually drips from the engine's rear.

So the mechanic, who through all the gunk accumulated under the engine can't really see where the drip is *originating* from, does a rear main seal replacement, when what's really needed is a simple top-engine gasket change out.

It happens in auto shops every day. Don't let it happen to you.

Even more confusing, if yours is a front-wheel drive, with the engine installed laterally, not front to rear, the engine's "rear" may not even be in the engine compartment's rear. And the sleuthing, while perhaps a mite easier, still isn't all that easy.

Complicating oil leak tracing is the ought-to-be obvious: when you are driving, road wind breezes beneath and around the engine (through the radiator grille, for example). Whiping past the engine, wind tends to pick up globules of oil, even oil coming from, say, the front engine timing cover gasket, and carries it back — again, making it appear as though the engine rear has sprung a leak.

You have probably seen cars with big blotches of oil on their rear deck lids or, if station wagons, smudging their closed tailgates. Vaguely, you may have wondered why. It's easily explained. In all likelihood, the smudges are wind-carried oil from the engine compartment. These cars — and the Corvairs and VWs seem special prey — create a particularly strong rear-end vacuum that conspires to catch the wind, flowing beneath the car, and divert it upward — upward and onto their rear decks.

If this road wind has picked up front-engine oil, it sticks to the vehicle's rear. The appearance? That the oil is coming from the rear of the vehicle. The opposite is often the fact.

Driveway drips certainly need investigation. And the worst of them must be sleuthed to their *source.*

Sleuthing, if you decide it needs doing, is something any good mechanic can do.

CAR-KEEPER'S DILEMMA: REPLACEMENT PARTS THAT NEED REPLACEMENT

Whether your car is 10 days or 10 years old, the problem's the same: you pick up the car after the mechanic has installed a new part, but the trouble hasn't been corrected. If it was hard to start before, it's still hard to start. If the water pump leaked, it still leaks. If the power steering didn't work, it still doesn't.

The mechanic's fault? Perhaps. Far more likely, however, what's at fault is the new or rebuilt (the so-called "exchange") part newly installed by the mechanic.

If they don't build cars as they used to (and they don't), it's for certain they don't build parts as they once did.

That they don't is one reason mechanics charge so much for parts replacement. Your mechanic knows what you may not: two or three parts may have to be installed until one works. And while parts suppliers credit (don't charge) the mechanic for returned faulty parts, they don't compensate his labor — the time he wastes installing one part after another until one finally works. Neither do parts suppliers compensate you, the car owner, for two or three trips to a shop to correct what should have been corrected with a first — and single — visit.

The author's experience over the past few years is, unfortunately, typical. On one occasion, a top-flight mechanic had to install three — count them, one, two, three — power steering pumps in as many days until one finally worked. On another occasion, two starter motors had to be installed the same day when the first was faulty.

Brand new factory parts fail as often and as readily as the rebuilts, which are often warranted "Good as

factory new." They should be warranted "No worse than factory parts."

Name the part — fuel pump, water pump, alternator, starter motor, power steering pump, and a dozen more — and your chances of getting a satisfactory replacement on the first try are seldom better than 80 percent: only about eight parts in every ten can be expected to work. Parts makers, of course, deny so high a failure rate. Mechanics and veteran car-keepers know otherwise.

Less veteran car-keepers too often fall prey to mechanics who, knowing only too well that a newly installed part doesn't work, insist that it does.

"That's the way it's supposed to work," the mechanic claims.

You know better. And you tell him so. His quick retort, "Lady, are *you* a mechanic?"

No, you are not. But you know if what was wrong is *still* wrong. You need not be a mechanic to *know* that — nor to insist, as you must, that the mechanic replace the part he has just installed with another that works. You tell him very firmly that you will not take the car, nor pay his bill, until he has satisfactorily corrected the problem. Almost certainly that will mean installation of yet another replacement part.

Some insight into the growing problem of replacement parts, which themselves need replacement, is found in Marvin Harris' provocative classic book, *"America Now, Why Nothing Works."* Why, asks Harris in analyzing why automobiles and their parts seldom seem to work right, should auto executives take seriously the consumers' complaints about their cars? After all, the auto executives' own cars — chauffeur-driven and serviced daily — work just fine.

YEARS-LONGER STRATEGY: ENGINE

Gasoline

1. Change oil whenever the oil is dirty, even if you had it changed only 500 miles before.
2. For regular, scheduled oil changes, follow your owner's manual's "severe driving" oil change mileage. (For engines, stop-and-go in-town driving is "severe.")
3. Use only top-grade (and never nondetergent) oil.
4. Have the engine professionally tuned every six months or approximately every 6,000 miles. (The every 12-months/12,000-miles tune-up recommended for average cars is not frequent enough for long-lived engine keeping.)
5. At every tune-up, or sooner if driving conditions indicate, have the air filter changed.

Diesel

1. Change oil whenever the oil is dirty, even if you had it changed only 500 miles before.
2. For regular, scheduled oil changes, follow your owner's manual's "severe driving" oil change mileage interval. *For most diesels, the oil should be changed every 3,000 miles.*
3. Use only diesel-grade, car-diesel recommended engine oil (see "What An Oil Can Can Tell You," page 140).
4. Change oil filter at *every* oil change.
5. Have air cleaner (filter) checked every 2,500–3,000 miles; replace every 15,000 miles.
6. Have fuel injectors checked/cleaned/adjusted every 15,000 miles.

Diesel engine's air filter must be checked more frequently than gasoline engine air filter because diesel takes in far greater volume of air.

7. If your engine does not now have one, have a water separator installed in the fuel system.
8. Fuel filters: have checked, cleaned at every 3,000-mile lube and lube-filter change. Replace fuel filters at 15,000 miles.

SYMPTOMS/CAUSES: GASOLINE ENGINE

Engine Won't Start or Starts Hard

Symptom

Won't start
(engine doesn't "crank" — turn over — but you may hear clicky sound)

Possible Cause

1. Battery weak or dead
2. Battery's terminals or cables corroded, loose, or broken
3. Starter system faulty
4. Ignition (key) switch has electrical short or defect
5. No fuel in tank

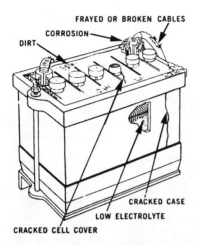

Six good reasons why your battery may not start your car. Among the most common: corrosion buildup on battery terminals. (Drawing courtesy of Fram Corporation.)

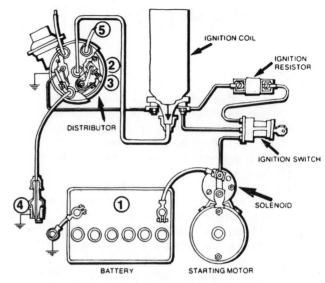

The starter-ignition system isn't all that complex. There are just a lot of parts that have to function correctly when you turn the key in the ignition switch—and one of the parts that has to work right is the ignition switch itself. (1) battery; (2) breaker points; (3) condenser; (4) spark plugs; (5) spark plug wires (harness). There is also the starting motor, its solenoid, the ignition resistor and ignition coil, and that ignition switch. (Drawing courtesy of Fram Corporation.)

The fuel system probably has more parts with which most car-keepers are familiar than any other system in your car: (1) air filter; (2) carburetor; (3) fuel filter; (4) vapor canister; (5) crankcase breather filter; plus the fuel pump and fuel line. (Drawing courtesy of Fram Corporation.)

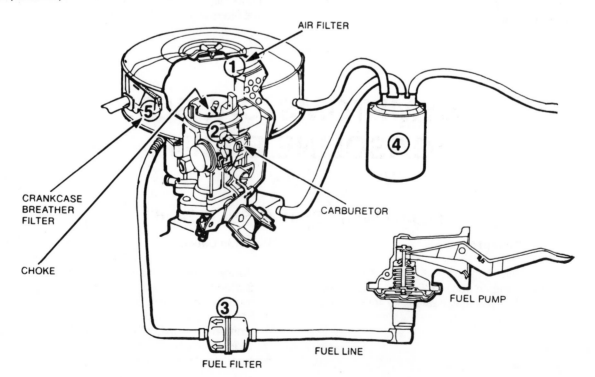

Symptom	Possible Cause
Won't start, but engine cranks slowly	1. Battery weak 2. Starter system problem 3. Electrical system problem
(in warm weather) Won't start, but cranks briskly	1. No fuel in tank 2. Improper starting procedure (you may have flooded engine) 3. Distributor or its points worn or defective 4. Fuel filter or line clogged 5. Fuel pump problem 6. Electronic ignition fault 7. Carburetor problem 8. Spark plug or spark plug cable problem
(in cold weather) Won't start, but cranks slowly	1. Battery weak 2. Engine's oil grade too heavy; congealed by cold
(in cold weather) Won't start, but cranks briskly	1. All as for warm weather above 2. Fuel system restriction, as ice
(in wet weather) Won't start, but cranks briskly (may hear crackling sound)	1. Spark plugs or their cables wet or shorting 2. Wet or cracked distributor cap or coil 3. Electronic ignition unit wet, moist, or shorting
Won't start; fuel odor when you crank engine	1. You have flooded engine 2. Choke defective 3. Carburetor problem 4. Fuel system problem
Starts, but stops or stalls when you turn ignition key from start position	1. Ignition switch or ignition system defective
Starts, but starts hard (requires excessive cranking)	1. Improper starting procedure (you may have flooded engine) 2. Choke malfunctioning 3. Spark plug, one or several, may not be firing 4. Distributor malfunctioning 5. Fuel system problem; too little fuel may be getting to carburetor 6. Tune-up indicated

SYMPTOMS/CAUSES: DIESEL ENGINE

Engine Won't Start or Starts Hard

Symptom	Possible Cause
Won't start (engine doesn't "crank"—turn over—but you may hear clicky sound)	1. Battery weak or dead 2. Battery's terminals or cables corroded, loose, or broken 3. Starter system defective 4. Seat belts not connected on "no start without belts" diesel cars 5. No fuel in tank
Won't start, but engine cranks slowly	1. Battery weak/terminals corroded 2. Improper starting procedure (see your owner's manual) 3. Glow plugs or glow plug system malfunctioning 4. Engine oil grade too heavy, congealed by cold
Won't start, but cranks briskly	1. No fuel in tank 2. Improper starting procedure (see your owner's manual) 3. Glow plugs or their system malfunctioning 4. Fuel contaminated (possible watered fuel problem) 5. Fuel injection problem
(in cold weather) Won't start, but cranks briskly	1. Wrong-grade fuel for cold weather; fuel congealing 2. No fuel in tank

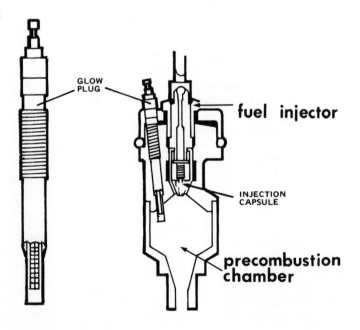

GLOW PLUG

fuel injector

INJECTION CAPSULE

precombustion chamber

Diesel fuel injectors and their capsules (nozzles) need to be checked, cleaned, and possibly replaced every 15,000 miles. Either a good diesel mechanic or an injector specialist can do it.

Note how glow plug, a kind of miniheater, preheats precombustion chamber. (Drawing courtesy of Caterpillar Tractor Co.)

Symptom	Possible Cause
	3. Improper starting procedure for cold weather (see your owner's manual)
	4. Glow plugs or their system malfunctioning
	5. Injection pump or fuel system malfunctioning
Starts, but idles roughly	1. Contaminated fuel
	2. Idle adjustment wrong
	3. Fuel system restriction
Starts, but idles roughly, with excessive smoke or noise	1. Injector nozzle(s) malfunction
	2. Injection pump timing problem
	3. Fuel contamination

SYMPTOMS/CAUSES: POOR FUEL ECONOMY

(Fewer Miles-Per-Gallon Than When Car Was Younger or Than Normal for Your Make and Model)

Symptom	Possible Cause
Poor fuel economy	1. Fuel-wasting bad driving habits
	2. Driving pattern change (you now do more in-town, less highway, driving)
	3. Driving locale change (you now drive at significantly higher altitudes)
	4. Aerodynamic change (e.g., addition of roof rack)
	5. Added power accessories
	6. Added weight (as a trailer)
	7. Engine tune-up neglected
	8. Excessive idling
	9. Fueling with lower octane gasoline
Noticeably declining fuel mileage	1. Tune-up neglected
	2. Tire inflation incorrect
	3. Engine losing compression
	4. Air cleaner dirty
	5. Carburetor problem
	6. Ignition system fault
	7. Timing setting incorrect
	8. Brakes dragging
	9. Wheel alignment fault
	10. Spark plugs faulty
	11. Fuel system malfunction or leak
	12. Exhaust system problem

WHAT AN OIL CAN CAN TELL YOU

Not all oil that comes out of the ground is the same. Neither is all oil that comes out of a can.

Engine oil is specially and very specifically compounded to do certain things and not to do others. If you drive diesel and add a can of oil meant for gasoline engines, you've added the *wrong* oil. If your car is gas-engined, pouring in diesel engine oil is equally wrong. And a car-keeper should *never* use a *non-detergent* oil, which means a non-engine-cleaning oil.

The oil can tells you to what specifications the oil has been compounded and for what engines the oil is intended. What tells you are the "oil codes." You'll find them on the top, and occasionally on the bottom, of the can. But in reading the codes you need to know the oil specification alphabet and what each letter or combination of letters means.

Oil codes beginning with *S* are for *gasoline engines*. Codes beginning with *C* are for *diesel engines*.

diesel lube oil specification codes

gas-engine lube oil specification code

Top-of-can oil codes show this is a top-grade engine oil for either gasoline or diesel engines.

GASOLINE ENGINE MOTOR OILS
Code

SF   New, improved, '80s, anti-engine-wear, and highly stable oil. Excellent for most gasoline engines.

SE   A "severe" duty oil, with excellent detergent, antirust, high-temperature stability. If you drive mostly in town and generally in stop-and-go traffic, use either the SE- or the newer SF-coded engine oils.

SD   A "severe" duty oil, which met car maker engine requirements for cars pre-1970. While it works for post-1970 gasoline engines, too, it is not the car-keeper's first or even second choice motor oil. Given the choice, choose either the SE- or SF-coded.

SC   Also a "severe" duty oil, but compounded to even older (1964–67) engine requirements. An "old code" oil, its specifications are outdated unless your engine is "old code," too.

SB   Another "old code" oil. Besides, this one is meant for "moderate" driving conditions, not for prolonged "severe" or stop-go driving.

SA   Skip this one altogether. It has few if any of the antirust, antiresidue, detergent qualities of the other *S* oils. Nor is the SA required to meet the tough specification requirements of the others. What's in an SA can is anybody's guess — your guess being as good as whoever sells it to you.

DIESEL ENGINE MOTOR OILS
Code

CD   A "severe" duty, excellent specification oil, able to withstand the modern diesel's high temperature and to protect, besides, against bearing corrosion and combustion deposits. Your first choice in diesel engine oils.

CC   A "moderate to light" duty diesel oil. Given the choice between the CD and CC, pick the CD every time.

CB   *Not* a good oil for diesel-engined cars. This one is more commonly used in industrial engines that burn high-sulphur fuels, and low-quality fuels at that. Also, it's recommended only for moderate service requirements.

CA   A "light duty" diesel engine oil, not recommended for diesel cars.

KNOCKING ENGINE KNOCK

What can you do about engine knock? The answer, from the experts, is straightforward: "You had better do something, or risk major engine trouble."

The knock problem is worsening for all cars, big or small, but in particular for many larger-engined, older kept cars with higher-compression engines.

When every service station pumped premium leaded, high-octane gasoline, the knock problem was easily solved. A car owner simply switched from lower octane regular to higher octane premium leaded gasoline. And, usually, that ended the engine's knocking. Now, however, high-octane premium leaded gas has all but disappeared from the pumps, leaving only the lower octane regular leaded and the regular and premium unleaded. None of these fuels may prevent knock in some higher-compression older engines.

There are two possible solutions if your engine persistently and intensively knocks. And while perhaps you aren't particularly interested in why it knocks, but rather in how to stop it from knocking, a few things are worth knowing about knock.

Basically, knocking occurs when there's an uncontrolled detonation of fuel in the combustion chamber. The fuel may detonate spontaneously, *before* the spark plug has had a chance to ignite the

fuel — and that is called *preignition knock*. Or, just as the fuel mix is ignited by the spark plug, a secondary fuel ignition in another area of the combustion chamber could be triggered. Created are two opposing flame fronts. When they collide — violently — you hear knock. This latter is called a *detonation knock*. Even experts can't tell you (without help from an electronic analyzer) which is which. But both are bad. And not just a little bad, but very bad.

Both of these uncontrolled explosions cause far more heat than normal. It is heat enough, particularly if the opposing flame fronts join and are directed toward the piston, to create a veritable blowtorch that can burn a hole right through the top of the piston.

The least desirable of today's two ways to get rid of fuel-caused engine knock is to have the engine *down-tuned* to run, without knocking, on today's low-octane no-leads or on low-octane leaded regular. Detuned, the engine won't knock, but it won't operate as efficiently as before. And your mileage is almost certain to downturn if you down-tune. Just how much fuel efficiency you lose depends on how much down-tuning the mechanic has to do.

The more desirable knock eliminator involves one of those car-keeping experiments where you can't lose. If it works, you're home free and knock-free. If it doesn't, you may have to go the down-tune route.

What makes the experiment fascinating is that involved is a phenomenon of physics called a *synergism:* In some instances, when *two* substances are mixed, the sum of their values is larger than their individual values. Thus, when you mix, let's say, one gasoline with a 90 octane rating and another with a 92 octane rating — and mix them 50/50 — you don't

Why engines knock—detonation knock: As fuel is compressed by piston into combustion chamber (1), it is ignited by spark plug (2) and combustion begins (3). But, a secondary combustion, self-ignited, begins in another area of combustion chamber (4). The two opposing flame fronts rush toward one another. They collide violently, causing knock you hear (5). (Drawings courtesy of Zollner Corporation.)

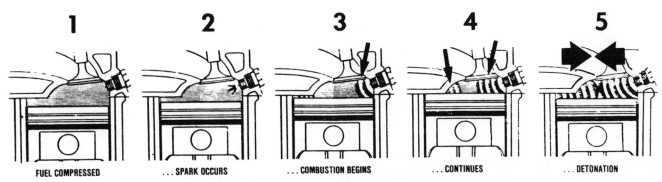

1	2	3	4	5
FUEL COMPRESSED	... SPARK OCCURS	... COMBUSTION BEGINS	... CONTINUES	... DETONATION

How Detonation happens—Detonation is a kind of follow-the-leader occurrence. Instead of just a single spark plug ignition of the piston's compressed fuel, other fuel ignition takes place opposite the spark plug in the remaining unburned fuel above the piston, and creates more than one flame front moving across the piston crown. When the opposing flame fronts meet, they explode and this detonation produces "engine knock".

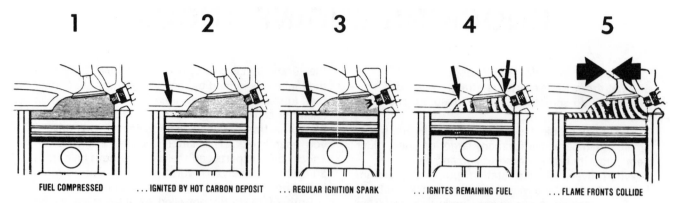

1 FUEL COMPRESSED
2 . . . IGNITED BY HOT CARBON DEPOSIT
3 . . . REGULAR IGNITION SPARK
4 . . . IGNITES REMAINING FUEL
5 . . . FLAME FRONTS COLLIDE

How Pre-ignition happens—Pre-ignition takes place when fuel combustion "jumps the gun". A portion of the piston's compressed fuel is ignited by excessive heat in the combustion chamber *before* the normal spark ignition takes place. When the flame fronts collide, the result is "engine ping".

Detonation and pre-ignition are so closely related that it's hard to distinguish between them. Close inspection of the damaged pistons is necessary to determine the exact cause of piston failure.

Why engines knock—preignition knock: As fuel is compressed by piston into combustion chamber (1), excessive heat ignites fuel charge before spark has fired (2). Spark then fires, igniting a second front of combustion (3). The two flame fronts rush toward one another (4) and collide violently (5), causing the knock you hear. (Drawings courtesy of Zollner Corporation.)

wind up with an octane rating in between (91 octane), but with an octane rating *higher* than either. Say, 95 octane or so.

The same phenomenon occurs, by the way, when propane gas is used to enhance the combustion of diesel fuel.

To see if synergism works for your knocking engine, next time you're in a service station buy *two* grades of gasoline. If you need 10 gallons, first pump in five gallons of the *highest-octane unleaded* gasoline the station offers. Then add five gallons of the station's *highest-octane leaded* gasoline. With this 50/50 mix (the recommended synergistic mix), the octane of the combined mix will be higher than that of either of the individual gasolines. And you may very well have solved your engine's knocking problem.

If not, try another station and a different brand of gasoline. Lead content of regular and the octane of the no-leads vary from brand to brand. You are almost certain — not 100-percent certain, but comfortingly close to it — to find, if you try enough brands, one that works synergistically for your engine.

And suddenly your high-compression knocker turns no-knock.

Glossary

Auto-dismantler: term preferred by auto wrecking and parts recovery places for what they do.

Belting: the usually three or more V-type belts, running on pulleys powered at the front of the engine, which drive various accessories or components, such as the radiator fan, generator or alternator, power-steering unit, water pump, air-conditioning compressor and others.

Bra: a car-front protective cover to prevent the finish, particularly front-end finish, from being nicked by rocks or other road debris.

Car cloth: fabric car upholstery material, as contrasted to vinyl upholstery material.

Car-keeping: the strategy of keeping a car operating longer and operating well.

Compression test: simple test of the compression in an engine's cylinders to determine if piston rings, valves, or both, need repair.

Crankshaft: the engine component that is powered by the cylinders' pistons and transmits that power, usually through transmission gearing, to the wheels. The crankshaft is the single engine component that is physically attached to or drives all other major engine components.

Customize: to personalize a kept car to fit a car-keeper's tastes and lifestyle.

Electrical harness: the set of electrical wires that power the spark plugs. The harness of a four-cylinder engine has four wires; of an eight-cylinder engine, eight wires.

Engine block: in an engine, the lower, power-producing part of the engine, which contains, among others, the cylinders, pistons, piston rings, and crankshaft.

Engine head: in an engine, the power-controlling bolt-on top part of the engine, which contains the cylinders' valves.

Five o'clock surprise: a larger than expected bill for car repairs handed the owner when, around 5:00 P.M., he picks up his car from the repair shop.

Fuel algae: micro-organisms that sometimes grow in diesel fuel and can usually be eliminated through use of a special fuel biocide.

Glitter lots: the used car lots of new car dealers in wealthy areas whose traded-in used cars have had exceptional care and maintenance.

H-pattern: in the rotation of radial-type tires, the front-to-rear tire-swapping pattern in which front tires merely trade places with the rear tires directly behind them.

Heat of compression: heat caused by the compression of air, within a cylinder's combustion chamber, by the piston. In a diesel engine, extremely high-compression heat spontaneously ignites the combustion chamber's fuel charge, without need of spark ignition, as in a gasoline engine.

Hydrometer test: in radiator maintenance, the simple test that tells how much antifreeze comprises the coolant mix and whether or not more should be added.

Iron: jargon for "automobiles," often used by car salesmen.

Kept car: a car kept longer than has been the practice of its owner.

Long block: in engine rebuilding or repair, the complete engine, including both its head and the block.

McPherson strut: a shock absorber that combines shock absorption action with a spring and is usually, unlike a standard shock absorber, an integral part of a car's steering-suspension systems.

Mileage interval: in car-keeping the approximate mileage before routine or necessary maintenance is required or anticipated.

Missing: in an engine, when one or more cylinders is no longer operating.

Naval jelly: a mild acid preferred by some for cleaning rust from car chrome.

On the hook: jargon for a tow job, when a car being towed by a tow truck is suspended from the truck's hook. A "hook" is no longer used in many towing situations today.

Polypenetrant: any of numerous car-keeping appearance products that both penetrate and luster car components, such as vinyl upholstery, vinyl roofs, tires, and various car moldings.

Pressure cap: a radiator cap designed to hold the radiator and its coolant under a higher pressure than they would normally be under at whatever altitude the car operates.

Remanufactured engine: an engine that is "factory rebuilt" as contrasted to being rebuilt by a mechanic in a repair shop.

Repacking: the lubrication, with grease, of the wheel bearings.

Self-stylist: a car-keeper who elects, within limits, to customize his car with various appearance items, such as a vinyl top, wheelcovers, striping, and the like.

Short block: in engine rebuilding or repair, only the top part, or head, of an engine, which contains the valves.

Strategy budget: in car-keeping, the amount of money a car-keeper budgets monthly for anticipated routine maintenance and updating of his kept car.

Strategy schedule: in car-keeping, the systematic scheduling by a car-keeper of maintenance or updating work that needs doing or is anticipated, in order to keep the car operating well and looking good for years and miles longer.

Turbocharging: the forcing of additional quantities of air, other than what an engine would naturally intake, into the combustion chambers of an engine, as an aid to better combustion, increased engine power, and fuel economy.

Valve and ring job: the replacement of an engine's piston rings and the grinding or machining, or replacement, of one or more of its valves, valve seats, or valve guides.

Wet sanding: in car repainting or retouching, the use—to achieve super smoothness in the finish—of a water-soaked, very lightly abrasive "sandpaper" (it is more often an emery grit paper).

Wheel balancing: corrective procedure for compensating for unavoidable manufacturing imbalance of tires, which may be out of balance or out of round.

Wheel cylinder: in drum-type brakes, the critical, plunger-type controller of hydraulic braking pressure, which powers the drum brakes' shoes and their brake linings when a car's brakes are applied.

Wheel weights: small, usually lead weights, used when balancing a wheel to correct any tire or wheel imbalance.

X-pattern: in the rotation of bias-type tires, the diagonal tire-switching pattern in which the left front tire trades places with right rear tire; the right front, with left rear.

Index